Goals Engineering

Design Your Success Plan

HAFFADH Hichem

Goals Engineering

By HAFFADH Hichem /ˈhæfæd ˈhiːʃəm/, Author & a Strategic Planner

For more information about this book or the author, please contact us at:

goalsengineering@outlook.com

Independently published

ISBN: 9798396917385

To use the template of this book for writers :

Free download by https://usedtotech.com

Contents

Dedication

To my beloved family, who have stood by me throughout my life,

To my esteemed life coach, Mr. Philippe Léveillé, for his unwavering support and guidance,

To all my friends who have shown me genuine love and respect,

To all the successful people who have inspired me and fueled my motivation to emulate them,

To every colleague who has believed in me,

And to everyone striving for success.

About the Author

Over the years, I have been studying the reasons behind my failures and successes, as well as the reasons behind the failures and successes of others. I have been constantly analyzing the subject and trying to find a solution to this puzzle.

It took me several years to prepare and condense this book. My daily routine, which serves as a compass for organizing my life, whispered ideas into my ear, while analyzing helped me comprehend and articulate this world through words. Intuition urged me to embrace clear and simplified approaches to planning. As an engineer, engineering terms naturally became the language in my mind for designing a system that would assist me in organizing my life and attaining my aspirations.

Consequently, I anticipate, or rather, I am confident that this book will revolutionize your outlook on success and goal attainment. It will acquaint you with your true self and equip you with an effective methodology for selecting, assessing, and achieving your goals.

Introduction

Whenever authors write books, they often allow themselves to go overboard with praise and admiration for their work, as if they were proud parents celebrating the achievements of their children who have grown and matured over the years. Following this tradition, I will now highlight the benefits of this book, but I will remain unbiased, just as I was during its creation. This book might truly be the best one you read about achieving goals and finding meaning in your life because it approaches this sensitive topic from a fresh perspective.

Most books that talk about success and goal achievement are motivational books, and it's rare to find a book that delves into the practical and actionable side of achieving goals. There are some books targeted towards businesses that help them achieve company goals through strategies backed by statistics. But why aren't there books that teach people how to create success as if it were a product, how to engineer their own destiny and have confidence that what they are doing will succeed?

Warning!

- This book overlooks the spiritual aspect of goal achievement.
- It may not motivate you to achieve your goals; in fact, it can sometimes be discouraging.
- It treats you as a mere machine with an improperly installed program, dismissing your existing knowledge about goal achievement as nonsense.
- While it may use engineering terms, it uses them figuratively and simplifies them to make them accessible to everyone.
- It helps you maintain logical thinking when selecting goals and rational planning.
- It doesn't provide a magical formula for goal achievement, but it presents the proper method for operating the system.

To ensure a deep understanding of every idea, it is important for you to read the book sequentially. Avoid rushing through the content, as this book requires you to sharpen your imagination and envision the interconnectedness of things. Read the book in order, allowing yourself to draw your own conclusions and uncover the process that suits you best, enabling you to achieve your goals.

Throughout the book, you may encounter tables, diagrams, and symbols. Take the time to read and contemplate them, as they may provide explanations that are even more valuable than the written text itself. However, it is essential to read everything in the order presented.

Sometimes, you will need a pen to answer some questions. If you're using an electronic version of this book, don't hesitate to write on external paper or use a dedicated writing application. I hope that you will find the idea of goal engineering an enjoyable and helpful method to understand the world of success.

GOALS ENGINEERING

HAFFADH Hichem

Chapter 1

The Power of Categorization

"Categorization is the essence of all human understanding"
Henri Poincaré

As human beings, we have a tendency to constantly desire and seek control over various things in life. The abundance of possibilities can often leave us feeling uncertain about what we truly want. This can be especially challenging when it comes to setting goals or deciding what we want for our future.

The difficulty in choosing what we want for ourselves in life doesn't solely arise from the abundance of possibilities. It also stems from our limited understanding of ourselves and our desires, some of which may have been suppressed in our subconscious minds since childhood. Moreover, humans often behave impulsively and irrationally, which can become a part of their decision-making process. Although they may sometimes try to use analytical thinking when making important decisions, they tend to rely on improvisation and going with the flow. This habit, combined with a lack of awareness of what they truly want, can lead to confusion when facing available choices and hinder their future success.

What motivates humans? Let's try to understand what drives them to take action or hold back. Are there numerous and varied motivators or are they limited and manifest in different ways? To be frank, there are only five motivators that make a person take action, and no more:

Money and Possession

The desire to possess material things is a powerful motivator that drives humans to exert effort. Money, in particular, holds a significant attraction for many of us, spurring us to work hard and strive to acquire more. This energy can be a driving force behind long, arduous endeavors. Some of us are willing to work for extended periods of time with the hope of obtaining it, while others take risks with the money they have earned.

In the pursuit of greater wealth, individuals, including criminals, often invest considerable time in meticulous planning and strategic maneuvers to acquire money, even in the face of inherent dangers. This powerful motivator not only activates the body's muscles, enabling them to endure pain and fatigue, but also stimulates the brain's cognitive processes, facilitating quick thinking and problem-solving. Simultaneously, it can evoke feelings of greed and an insatiable desire for more.

Health and Safety

Let's face it, good health is something we all desire and hold dear. It's a different kind of energy from the driving force of money; in fact, it's more of a regulator. While our desire for wealth demands physical and mental exertion, our yearning for good health strives to keep that exertion in check. We aim to steer clear of anything that could harm our bodies and avoid fatigue or injury. It's this fear of losing our health that holds us back and guides our actions, as we strive to strike a balance between effort and rest.

This force also serves as an expert filter and purifier. Our desire for health dictates what we consume, what activities we engage in, and what we avoid to prevent illness and disease. Sometimes it urges us to move, prompting us to exercise and work towards a leaner and fitter body or to invest in our wellbeing through medical consultations or herbal remedies.

Emotions and Well-being

The driving force we refer to as happiness is a complex psychological state that we all crave and seek to experience. It fuels our desire to explore the causes of these emotions and indulge in activities like listening to music, meditating, fun or even engaging in harmful behavior like drug use.

This powerful driving force impacts every aspect of our being and affects the other engines that drive us forward. Whether we call it spirituality, emotions, or happiness, the name doesn't matter. What's important is that it encompasses all activities, goals, and expectations related solely to the self and how it feels.

The primary role of this driving force is to charge the battery and supply creative energy. Without a satisfied soul, the other engines can't function properly. Each engine plays a vital role in allowing the others to function, as money allows us to fulfill emotional needs, nourish the body, and maintain good health. In turn, good health contributes to earning money and brings contentment to the self.

Knowing and Understanding

Humans are naturally inclined to curiosity, and it's what drives us to learn new things. While some people may have a tendency to be lazy about learning, we tend to be motivated by things that catch our interest or that are necessary for solving problems. This driving force compels us to search, train, and acquire the skills we need to achieve our goals. It's essential because the other engines of motivation can only function properly with accurate and abundant information. This engine serves as a roadmap for the other engines to follow, and without it, finding what we want can be challenging and reliant on luck alone.

Relations and Reputation

The connections we have with others play a significant role in shaping our actions and behaviors. Our innate desire to maintain relationships drives us to comply with certain expectations or even make sacrifices, showcasing the immense power of social bonds as a fundamental driving force. The allure of fame, the desire for a large social circle, and the need to prove oneself to others all stem from the existence of other people in our lives.

The engine of relations is fueled by our need for connection and the desire to find a place among others. It compels us to take actions that bring us closer to official or personal entities, fostering a sense of belonging and social validation.

Are There Other Categories ?

There are countless ways to classify human motivations, but such categorization is of little use. What we really crave is simplicity and clarity. Rather than needlessly subdividing human nature into various categories, it is better to comprehend ourselves in a straightforward manner, enabling everyone to benefit from this understanding. The five primary motivators that we have discussed serve this purpose well. To confirm this, consider any activity or goal that comes to mind; it will certainly fall within one of these categories.

Do you aspire to become a millionaire? The intense drive behind this goal stems from a love of money and material possessions, which falls under the financial motivator we identified earlier. Do you long for adventure and traveling around the world? This is driven by the motivational force of the soul or spirit, which draws positive feelings. And if you desire to build a lean, muscular physique, this is motivated either by a love of your own body or a desire to exhibit strength to someone else. In other words, the motivators of health and relations are at work, either individually or together.

It's common for us to have multiple motivations for a certain action, but there is always one that has a stronger impact than the others. It's as if these engines can't all operate at full speed simultaneously, so one of them takes the lead role while the others temporarily slow down or become less influential until another goal arises.

Later on, we will delve into the relationship that links these categories, but in summary, these five motivators work together harmoniously to create a unique blueprint within each individual that pertains to success and goal achievement. However, if they are misused or misdirected, they can have negative consequences and lead to traps and difficult situations.

The Categorisation Technique

"Without a classification of the objects we perceive, our cognition would be an unbounded, chaotic process of grasping similarities and differences." - Eleanor Rosch

When it comes to setting goals, there are five driving forces that influence our decisions and choices: wealth, health, emotions, knowledge, and relations. Each of these engines has a unique impact on our character and personality, and they work together in varying intensities to shape our goals and aspirations.

By categorizing our goals into these five templates, we take the first step towards self-understanding and gain clarity on our expectations, actions, and deeds. This approach is a practical way to track our progress and take control of our lives.

For instance, let's consider a list of goals and attempt to classify them into the corresponding categories. This exercise will help us comprehend the underlying motives and significance of pursuing these goals.

- I want to set up an e-commerce company.
- I want to visit the Canary Islands.
- I want to play chess smartly.
- I want to be cured of eczema.
- I want to learn to play the violin well.
- I want to get rid of anxiety in my life.
- I want to set up a charity.
- I want to lose weight.
- I want to buy a plot of land.
- I want to get a job with a higher salary
- I want to get married and have children
- I want to watch the funniest comedy.

To gain a better understanding of your aspirations and ensure that your life is balanced, start by listing all your goals and aspirations on a piece of paper. Then, categorize each goal based on what you have learned about the five engines that drive an individual's choices.

It's important to keep in mind that some goals may fit into multiple categories, so choose the one that is most suitable. This process is essential in understanding the true motivation behind your goals and engineering them effectively.

Learning to play an instrument or acquiring new skills and knowledge fall under cognitive goals, while building a family or creating an association is driven by our desire to find a place among people and improve our social status. By classifying your goals in this way, you can gain a deeper understanding of your inclinations and make sure that you live a well-balanced life.

"Classification is necessary in order to simplify and clarify complex phenomena." - Thomas Henry Huxley

Money category goals

- Set up an e-commerce company.
- Buy a plot of land.
- A job with a higher salary.

Health category goals

- Be cured of eczema.
- Lose weight.

Feeling category goals

- Visit the Canary Islands.
- Get rid of anxiety.
- Watch a funny comedy.

Learning category goals

- Play chess smartly.
- Play the violin well

Relations category goals

- Set up a charity.
- Get married and have children

The solution to goal-setting may differ among individuals since we each have a unique genetic imprint related to our goals. While there may be agreement on the fundamental categories, there may be variations in the details. Therefore, it's acceptable to have some differences in our approach to this solution.

As a follow-up to this exercise, create a list of twenty goals or activities that you genuinely desire to achieve and classify them using the five categories we discussed earlier.

Don't worry about whether they're achievable or not; that's a different matter we'll address later. Write down everything you want, as they come to your mind.

Money category goals

- ....
- ....
- ....
- ....

Health category goals

- ....
- ....
- ....
- ....

Feeling category goals

- ....
- ....
- ....
- ....

Knowing category goals

- ....
- ....
- ....
- ....

Relations category goals

- ....
- ....
- ....
- ....

Once you've classified your goals based on their underlying motives, take a moment to reflect on how it makes you feel. Do certain categories weigh more heavily on you than others? This is an essential step in goal engineering, as it helps to uncover the reasons behind our desires, actions, and habits.

For example, if you prioritize financial goals over feeling goals, you may be the type of person who strives for financial freedom and wealth at the expense of your own comfort. On the other hand, if you value mental comfort and happiness more than money, you may be someone who enjoys life and lives in the moment.

In the next chapter, we will delve deeper into the five major motivators and analyze how they stack up for you. By breaking down goals into smaller components and approaching them like engineering problems, you'll learn how to achieve any goal.

CHAPTER 2

The Magic of Ranking

"When you rank things, you make choices that keep you on the right path and help you climb higher." - John C. Maxwell

In this chapter, we will explore the magic of ranking when it comes to achieving your goals. However, before diving into this topic, it's important to have a solid understanding of the principle of categorization. If it's been a while since you last read the book, we recommend revisiting the previous chapter to refresh your memory. Once you have a good grasp of the general idea, you can return to this chapter for a deeper dive into the interconnected concepts of goal engineering.

If we categorize our goals, we can see how they relate to each other and what they have in common. However, ranking our goals directly reveals why we favor some things over others. For example, if you spend most of your time on social media looking for new connections and struggle, dislike or ignore learning, then your motivation for relationships is stronger than your motivation for knowledge.

To use the ranking method more effectively, we won't rank our goals according to priority, like many people do with their New Year's resolutions. Instead, we will rank the five motivators we learned about in the previous chapter to understand why we prioritize certain things. You'll soon find out why.

Imagine with me the following list of goals :

- I want to save $10,000 within months.
- I want a profitable investment with a 10% return.
- I want to overcome depression.
- I want to sustain my meditation practice.

You can prioritize and determine which goal is more important to you by ranking them, but this may not be practical for a long list of goals. It's important to note that some goals may be similar and fall under the same category or family, making ranking them redundant as they have the same underlying motive. By organizing goals into groups and families, you can gain a clearer understanding of which of the five motivators is more influential for you and with what intensity, relative to the other motivators.

As you rank these five categories, a pattern or a unique imprint will emerge that distinguishes you, enabling you to scrutinize any given goal. You'll discern whether it's genuinely one of your authentic aspirations or if you're merely emulating someone else's notion of triumph.

If you gravitate towards knowledge type goals and strive to enhance your intellect, that's your benchmark of accomplishment. Conversely, accumulating a vast sum of money constitutes success for others who differ from you. Arranging goals according to groups and families will stratify individuals based on their predilections and temperaments, deepening our comprehension of why we pursue specific actions and how we persevere in the face of minor challenges.

Methods of Ranking

How can we use mathematical principles to rank these five categories and the intensity of our attachment to them? There are three main methods that we will adopt in this book:

- Direct traditional ranking
- Ranking through a psychological test
- Ranking through long-term observation

The first two methods involve direct and rapid evaluations, and they are considered accurate because they are spontaneous and straightforward. The third method, on the other hand, requires months of observation and is not as precise because it involves evaluation and introspection, making it useful mainly for confirming and monitoring results obtained from the direct methods in the long run.

Let's examine each method individually and explore how it can be utilized to obtain a genetic code that sets you apart from others.

The Traditional Direct Method

This method relies on a direct and superficial ranking of the five engines in a purely mathematical manner. When someone poses the question, "Do you value money or health more?" They are applying this method, which presents a simplified criterion for comparison but is inherently profound.

While most people may answer that health is more important than money due to the widely held belief that money cannot buy good health, the reality is far more complex. For some individuals, the wealthy are perceived as being healthier than the less affluent due to their access to top-tier medical facilities and expensive healthy eating options. Moreover, the financial security that wealth provides can significantly reduce the likelihood of developing health complications. Hence, although some may not explicitly express it, they believe that money holds a certain degree of importance and the ability to actually buy some health.

When comparing words, we rely on certain criteria. First, we consider the importance of each word to us by asking which is more significant. Then, we examine our personal desires and inclinations to determine which word we prefer. Lastly, we look at how these words are embodied in our daily lives and which ones drive our actions and behaviors. Using these criteria, we can create a comprehensive table to compare the five words and organize them based on their relevance. This table encompasses all possible comparison scenarios, making it easy for us to evaluate and make informed decisions.

You have a scoring range of 1 to 20 for evaluating each side of the equation, which aligns with the number of available cells for scoring.

It's important to avoid assigning the same score to both items, as that wouldn't make logical sense. For example, if you're comparing money with health, it wouldn't be appropriate to give them equal weight. If money is extremely important to you, give it a score of 20 and assign a different score to health.

Remember that the score you give to one item is allocated and can't be used again in the next rows of the table. Keep in mind the importance of the word in your practical life, not just your personal desire, and make sure to remain neutral in your decision-making process.

Left-hand side	Left-hand side SCORE	right-hand side	Right-hand side SCORE
Money		Health	
Money		Emotions	
Money		Knowledge	
Money		Relations	
Health		Emotions	
Health		Knowledge	
Health		Relations	
Emotions		Knowledge	
Emotions		Relations	
Knowledge		Relations	

Here's a tip: If you assign 20 points to money when comparing it to health, you can't allocate those same 20 points to compare money with another engine. Remember, no two engines carry the same weight or influence. Some of the engines will receive a lower score because all the available scores have been used up.

Gather the points garnered for each word, being mindful not to overlook any column. There exist four columns allocated to each word. It is essential to avoid assigning the same score to two words, lest the system be rendered inoperative. In the event of such an occurrence, it implies indecisiveness and failure to differentiate between the two words. A reevaluation of the criteria employed is advised.

Engine	Total score
Money	
Health	
Emotions	
Knowledge	
Relations	

After obtaining the total score for each engine, you can arrange the words in descending order, from the highest to the lowest, based on the score obtained. This order represents your genetic fingerprint related to success. Remember this order well because it will build many things in this book

Ranking	Engine name
1st	
2nd	
3rd	
4th	
5th	

"Ranking is not just for sports or academics, it is an essential tool for making decisions in life. Without ranking, we are left with a chaotic world where everything has equal importance and no direction." - John C. Maxwell

Psychological Test Ranking

The traditional way of ranking based on direct comparison may not be straightforward because it's challenging to capture the full meaning of a word when comparing, and the answer isn't typically intuitive. Instead, we may need to delve into the unconscious by posing questions that force the individual to make a critical decision on which situation they prefer.

This approach ensures the results are more accurate. Psychological tests work on the same principle as traditional mathematical comparisons, but they conceal the comparison process and prompt the user to focus on the situation at hand.

The evaluation method via a psychological test is straightforward. You simply read the situation and respond candidly, even if you're uncomfortable with it. The more spontaneous you are, the more accurate your answer is, while overthinking may lead to doubts. However, don't worry, as these instances occur when the difference between both sides of the situation is slight, making comparison a challenging task.

In this situation, recall similar instances from your past and use them to support your answer. Nevertheless, it's best to answer candidly and with a general mindset. When you encounter a situation, evaluate it by assigning a numerical value to it:

Evaluation	Meaning
4 pts	This statement is entirely accurate and relevant to me.
3 pts	It is partially true, but not entirely accurate.
2 pts	I'm not convinced that it's true, I have doubts.
1 pt	While it may occur on occasion, it is not entirely accurate.
0 pts	This is completely false, as I rarely experience this.

Situation 1:

The manager requests the employees to put in extra hours because of the increase in demand, and promises to triple the hourly wage for those who do so.

A- I will push through even though I'm tired to earn the extra money and maybe even earn recognition for my dedication......pts

B- I'm exhausted and in need of rest. Would the extra money be worth it if I end up getting sick from overworking?......pts

Situation 2:

A- I am saving money for emergencies. I may get sick someday and I will have nothing but my own money to rely on......pts

B- I must buy supplements, healthy food, and medications in a timely manner. I may spend a lot of money, but this will preserve my health when I need it......pts

Situation 3:

A- I plan on buying inexpensive fruits and vegetables to save money with each purchase. Over time, I'll accumulate a lot of savings just by managing my expenses well and taking advantage of opportunities.......pts

B- Since I'm not aware of the amount of toxins and chemicals present in conventional vegetable markets, I'll opt for organic fruits and vegetables instead. Health regulatory organizations ensure that they are naturally grown.......pts

Situation 4:

A - Despite the great risks involved in investing in the stock market, the profit resulting from it is worth it.......pts

B - I prefer to invest in banks or safe bonds. I cannot keep up with the fast fluctuations of stocks and currencies and I feel short of breath. I don't want to have a heart attack just because of that excessive excitement.......pts

Situation 5:

A- Although I would love to go to this movie screening, it's just too pricey.......pts

C- I've been anticipating this movie for so long, I can't let this opportunity slip away.......pts

Situation 6:

A- How much does a trip to the Maldives cost? ......pts

C- I will put all my savings into this enjoyable trip to the Maldives.......pts

Situation 7:

A- I'll pray for God to bless me with abundant wealth during my prayers........pts

C- I'll pray and talk to God, sharing all my worries and emotional problems that are bothering me........pts

Situation 8:

A- The deceitful often outsmart the greedy, so it's important to be cautious of fraud and scams........pts

C- Why is it that my emotions wield such overpowering control over me, compelling me to indulge in avarice and acquire everything in sight, despite the numerous occasions on which I have fallen victim to deceit as a consequence?........pts

Situation 9:

A- I'm determined to finish this project, I anticipate it will be lucrative and I'm willing to put in the effort to make it successful no matter the cost........pts

D- Before embarking on this project, I need to carefully analyze all its facets and identify the skills required for its success. Planning is crucial before commencing. Nonetheless, I won't lose anything. I will have gained knowledge even if the project fails due to unfortunate circumstances........pts

Situation 10:

A- What's the point of learning this skill if it doesn't bring in money?.......pts

D- I really like this field! I will explore it in my free time........pts

Situation 11:

A- This training course is very expensive, isn't it? ......pts

D- This course is worth its weight in gold. It's okay to put some of my savings into it, I will benefit a lot.......pts

Situation 12:

A- When I become rich, people will know then that I am smart......pts

D- When I become smarter and people know that, I will become richer.......pts

Situation 13:

A: Why are we expected to bear the high cost of this tax stamp and pay a hefty sum for a residency document? It seems like there's no way out........pts

E: Finally, I have resolved my documentation issue. Ah, now I feel free as long as I am in a legal situation........pts

Situation 14:

A- Although I don't like the current mayor of this city, if I pretend to be loyal, I might be able to secure a big project and make a fortune........pts

E- I aspire to become the mayor of this city. While I will strive to maintain my honesty, this position will afford me many opportunities, including official relationships and access to powerful people. Perhaps one day I could even become the president of the country. Why not dream big? ....pts

Situation 15:

A- I have to become rich to help my family.......pts

E- I may not have a lot of money, but standing by my family and loving them sincerely will make me respectable to them and everyone else........pts

Situation 16:

A- I believe that once I achieve financial success, my ideal partner will be drawn to me, even if they initially have reservations. Over time, my wealth will help them understand and appreciate the love I have to offer.........pts

E- I desire a relationship founded on genuine affection rather than superficial possessions.........pts

Situation 17:

B- I will refrain from smoking, drinking alcohol, and consuming those toxins. Not only are they detrimental to my health, but they will also diminish my long-term happiness..........pts

C- I know smoking and drinking may be harmful, but there's a certain pleasure in indulging in those toxins that I just can't resist.........pts

Situation 18:

B- Although running can be tiring, it has benefits for blood circulation.........pts

C- While running outdoors is beneficial to health, if you don't find it pleasurable, there's no need to force yourself to do it.

Situation 19:

B - Taking a cold water shower is beneficial for immunity and many other things, as the doctor said. He even recommends it during winter cold days! ......pts

C - Swimming is enjoyable. Showers should be hot in winter and the pool lukewarm in summer.......pts

Situation 20:

B- Intermittent fasting is beneficial for health and also improves mood.......pts

C- Enjoying a delicious meal improves mood.......pts

Situation 21:

B- I have faith in what this doctor is saying because I have tried it myself and it worked.......pts

D- I won't trust what this doctor is saying until he can convince me scientifically. I want to understand, given my strong background in biology, I could even become a doctor myself if I wanted to. The fact is, we can learn anything.......pts

Situation 22:

B - This medication is effective.......pts

D - What are the ingredients of this medication? I'll read the prescription, and if I don't understand, I can search on the internet.......pts

Situation 23:

B - Bodybuilders develop their muscles through consistent exercise and a rigorous health regimen, requiring both courage and patience.......pts

D - Simply eating well and exercising is not enough to build muscle; professional guidance from a trainer who provides scientifically-based advice is essential........pts

Situation 24:

B - Natural ointments offer superior efficacy compared to synthetic ones and provide a higher level of safety.......pts

D - What factors could make chemical ointments potentially harmful? How can we mitigate these risks and ensure that they are on par with the quality of natural ointments? ......pts

Situation 25:

B - Although I enjoy interacting with those reckless boys, I'm apprehensive that they may instill in me some bad habits such as drug use or other hazardous practices, hence I tend to steer clear of them.......pts

E - These boys might have a wild side, but I'm confident that I can manage them without jeopardizing my own safety. Moreover, it's crucial for me not to portray myself as too dissimilar from them to avoid creating a social divide.......pts

Situation 26:

B - When I go to a party, I am bothered by the amount of sugar, cooking oils, alcohol and harmful substances that I have to consume.......pts

E - The party is an excellent opportunity for me to meet new people.......pts

Situation 27:

B - When I'm feeling energetic, I can run and exercise for an extended period.......pts

E - Running with the encouragement of friends or even strangers always makes me feel like I am part of a team, rather than just running alone.......pts

Situation 28:

B- Beautification and adornment make me look younger and healthier........pts

E- Beautification and adornment will bring me greater opportunities to find a partner.......pts

Situation 29:

C - I love music........pts

D - I want to learn and master music........pts

Situation 30:

C - The law of attraction works and achieves results if it is associated with strong emotions.........pts

D - Does the law of attraction really work or is it just a myth? How does it work then?........pts

Situation 31:

C - I prefer to enjoy myself first and then focus on my studies........pts

D - I make sure to study enough before I go have fun and unwind.........pts

Situation 32:

C - I feel a strange but wonderful feeling........pts

D - Why do I feel this way? What happened or what did I go through that caused this feeling?.......pts

Situation 33:

C - I find hiking in nature enjoyable and it brings me great peace of mind........pts

E - Hiking in nature with good company makes me feel part of the group........pts

Situation 34:

C - Worshiping is beneficial because it's comforting for the soul........pts

E - When we go to places of worship, we meet people we love and share activities with them........pts

Situation 35:

C - Even if I can't physically help people because I have other things to do, I still wish them well........pts

E - Just sitting with people, listening to them and sharing their experiences is a form of help........pts

Situation 36:

C - When I engage in charity work, I feel a wonderful sense of satisfaction........pts

E- My involvement in charity work, such as building an association, will earn me respect among people. I don't seek praise from them all the time, but I know that such actions make them happy and raise my value in their eyes........pts

Situation 37:

D- Effective communication and meaningful interactions with people necessitate acquiring a wide range of knowledge, including an understanding of human nature, psychology, and various interpersonal skills.........pts

E - While it's important for me to maintain spontaneity in my communication, I should also approach others with care and be mindful of my words to avoid hurting their feelings..........pts

Situation 38:

D - Why do societies behave this way...? ....pts

E - Diplomacy and good communication are the best ways to navigate and control societal anger.........pts

Situation 39:

D - Leaders need to learn politics and its intricacies to be successful...........pts

E - A leader should possess natural skills in politics and dealing with people, which doesn't necessarily require years of college education.........pts

Situation 40:

D - I need to study the personality of my partner to know how to deal with them...........pts

E - I should show love and politeness to my partner to make their love for me genuine.........pts

We apologize for the large number of questions, but it is necessary for the diagnosis. In fact, we need a large number of questions, and the more questions we have, the more accurate the diagnosis will be.

You may have noticed that the situations are categorized into groups according to letters. Sum up the points obtained for each letter, and be careful not to overlook any during the counting process. It is crucial to ensure that there are 16 repetitions for each letter, so that your calculation is accurate.

Finally, record the results in the provided table.

A	B	C	D	E
Total score ....pts	Total score ....pts	Total score ....pts	Total score ....pts	Total score ....pts

Legend :

A. Acquiring physical wealth, possessions, money, and accomplishing tangible goals.
B. Health, safety , vitality and youth.
C. Emotions, happiness, joy and feeling good.
D. Curiosity, learning and understanding.
E. Reputation, cultivating relationships, and coexisting within the community.

After counting and calculating, you can rearrange the categories again according to the score obtained for each category.

Ranking	Engine name
1st	
2nd	
3rd	
4th	
5th	

Once you have completed the counting and calculations, it is possible to rearrange the categories based on the scores obtained for each category. It is expected that you will obtain the same ranking that you obtained through the direct traditional method. This is because both methods are built on the same principles. If there is a significant difference in rankings, it means that you were not truthful in your answers and were selecting what you preferred instead of what truly reflects you.

There is no harm in retaking the test at a later time if you want to confirm the ranking of the five categories. Moreover, if you comprehend the underlying mechanism, feel free to create your own tests. Essentially, we are simply comparing engines by questioning the genuine reason behind a particular action. This approach can even be applied to the simplest activities in your daily life, such as doing laundry. Are you washing your clothes to eliminate germs and safeguard yourself from itching, or are you doing it to appear clean to others and avoid strange looks? It is crucial to be honest with yourself while making this comparison and take sufficient time to reflect on the ranking of these engines within yourself.

"Psychological tests are like X-rays for the mind, providing insight into the hidden aspects of ourselves." - Brian Tracy

Using a psychological test can help determine the order of your five engines. It's important to regularly reassess the sequencing of these engines, as they form the foundation of your journey towards success. While the psychological test shouldn't be the sole criterion, it serves as an effective tool for engaging with your unconscious mind. Engaging in introspection and deliberate self-analysis allows you to uncover your inherent tendencies through self-dialogue. Dedicate a portion of each day to reflect on your true aspirations, while maintaining a healthy skepticism towards your mind's responses.

Long-term Observation

Once you have obtained your personal code, which represents the order of the five categories, you can verify its accuracy in your daily life. It is important to keep a close eye on your daily actions and significant decisions that shape your life. When you become aware of what you are doing, take a moment to reflect on the reason that motivated you to take that particular action. Which of your inner engines or motivations was at work at that moment? Jotting down your observations in a notebook and monitoring their development over time can be a helpful practice.

What others say about you can also provide insights into your category ranking. If people describe you as stingy, it may indicate that you place a high value on money and fear losing it more than anything else, thus placing it in a high rank on your five-category scale (actually it occupies the 3rd rank as will be seen in the 5th chapter).

Conversely, if someone were to tell you that you have an obsession with cleanliness or an excessive fear of toxic foods and are overly concerned with your health, this is a clear indication that you prioritize your health and consider it a high priority.

Daydreams and dreams can also shed light on one's self-awareness. If you repeatedly dream about finding money hidden under your pillow, this may suggest that you value money greatly and have an unexpressed desire to possess it. Although the observation method may seem vague, it can be useful in verifying the results obtained through other more quantitative methods. Ultimately, it is a powerful tool for gaining a practical understanding of oneself.

It might take a considerable amount of time to rank your five engines, and the more mistakes you've made in the past, and the more you've tried to emulate others' success, the more challenging it becomes to figure out your true desires. It's completely alright to invest a significant period in self-reflection, truly understanding yourself, and delineating the authentic goals you are meant to pursue. Because if you fail to fulfill your role in life, you will never experience a sense of fulfillment, and you won't be able to say, "Now I can peacefully depart, having accomplished everything I wished for," before you pass away.

Chapter 3

Code Analysis

Once you have obtained your personal code, which represents the order of the five categories, incorporate it into your identity, either by writing it down or committing it to memory, just like you would remember your own name. This code reflects your genetic makeup in terms of success and achieving your goals.

Now, let us delve into the topic of analysis and understanding how the order of the engines from one individual to another influences their performance and the goals they pursue.

The primary engine, which holds the first rank in any order, exerts the greatest influence over a person's decision-making and goal-setting processes. If money is your primary engine, you are likely to find it necessary to pursue it relentlessly, and may not feel as tired or exhausted in the pursuit of it, as someone whose primary engine is health or feelings for example. Such an individual is less likely to exhaust themselves in the pursuit of wealth.

The primary engine is like the mother tongue of an individual, a deeply ingrained desire that drives them to set goals and engage in activities. But why do we sometimes not feel the direct impact of this strong primary engine? The reason is the relationship it has with the engine ranked second, which we'll call the brakes or competing engine.

The second rank serves to temper the primary driving force and bring equilibrium to a person's life. For example, if someone's primary focus is "Money," indicating that their greatest motivation is the pursuit of wealth, and "Health" occupies the second position, this individual will be highly ambitious in their quest for financial success while also prioritizing their safety.

This creates a stark contrast in their life as they strive to work hard for money while also conserving energy to prioritize their health. It is not a contradiction but rather a delicate balance that may result in successful entrepreneurs dedicating only a few hours each day to money-making pursuits, with the remainder of their time devoted to rest and taking care of their bodies.

The primary engine that drives us all is our deep-seated desires and inherent mindset, which compel us to set goals and engage in activities that we may not even acknowledge to ourselves. This applies not only to money and health, but also to other important aspects of life.

For instance, if knowledge were in the second rank instead of health, a person would still work hard for money, but would also be keen on learning, which would temper their ambition for wealth. They prioritize their learning endeavors, creating a balance in their lives and leading them to undertake projects not solely for monetary gain but also for personal development. They are inclined to pursue their goal of becoming and staying intelligent and analytical, which prevents them from doing anything foolish solely for the sake of earning money.

The third rank in this hierarchy may be less powerful than the first and second ranks, but it can be considered the most important and dangerous engine of all. Suppose a person's hierarchy of goals is as follows:

1. Money
2. Health
3. Emotions

In this scenario, the individual may be driven to pursue wealth and plan projects, while also being conscious of their health. However, as we have mentioned earlier, their focus on health may lead them to conserve their energy and avoid physically demanding work. Furthermore, the third rank engine of emotions could compel them to prioritize their emotional well-being, leading them to make decisions that may not necessarily be in their best interest in terms of financial or physical health.

The third rank is the one that truly determines a person's type. When the Emotion engine is positioned in the third rank, it signifies that the individual strives for emotional stability and happiness, but to a lesser extent than their desire for wealth and health.

The placement of these engines in this specific order can cause this “entrepreneur” to yield to their desire for emotional stability and avoid exposing themselves to strong emotions like feeling endangered or experiencing changes in circumstances, which could decrease their willingness to take risks. That is why the third rank in the classification system is known as the "Comfort Zone", as it obstructs a person from attaining the goals of the first and second ranks by adding an extra burden to them.

This rank doesn't necessarily have to be related to the Emotion engine. If the man mentioned in the previous example has the Knowledge engine in the Comfort Zone, which is the third rank, he will attempt to rationalize his failure to achieve goals by saying that he is still learning and is content with that. It may still seem intricate at this point, but we will provide more examples later on and elucidate more clearly why this rank should be referred to specifically as the Comfort Zone.

In times of necessity, humans turn to the fourth rank, which is weak and insignificant, but they still have some desire to improve it, albeit with a weak drive and a lack of enthusiasm.

The actions associated with this rank are not typically pursued as goals, but rather are temporary measures used by humans in times of need. This is why we refer to this rank as the basic tool, as it serves only to provide temporary assistance.

While each rank on the scale serves the rank above it, the first three ranks are all about setting and achieving goals, whereas the fourth rank does not have many goals of its own. Instead, it provides actions and tools to help individuals achieve the goals of the higher ranks on the scale. For instance, in the previous example, a person might have the following order:

1. Money
2. Health
3. Emotions
4. Knowledge

According to our assessment, this individual is more inclined to pursue career advancement than to complete projects. Even if they do attempt a project, taking significant risks is more challenging for them than it is for other entrepreneurs. As a result, they prioritize safety and their comfort zone, which is an extremely precarious position.

The knowledge engine ranks fourth on the scale. This suggests that they avoid spending time and energy and do not prioritize learning in the same way that those higher up on the scale do. Instead, they only use knowledge as a tool in difficult situations where money is at stake. As an employee, they do not prioritize learning new skills, instead preferring to improvise. By neglecting direct learning, they naturally lean towards creativity and inventing things from scratch, rather than learning pre-existing skills that may be burdensome. This can sometimes leave them stuck in tasks that bring in money directly, if only they had learned how to do them. This represents a significant limitation to their progress and may lead to failure if they do not develop their cognitive abilities, which are a weak point for them.

Finally, the fifth rank on the scale, also known as the blind spot, is a significant weakness for this individual. It is both faded and undesirable. This rank is characterized by a chaotic array of wishes, unclear and postponed plans, and sometimes repressed inclinations that the individual may not even be aware of.

In the previous example:

1. Money
2. Health
3. Self
4. Knowledge
5. Relations

The individual possessing this particular set of characteristics lacks an interest in developing relations, meeting new people, or striving to stand out and compete among them. This introverted nature tends to leave them with few friends and unwilling to engage in social activities or seek the spotlight. However, in times of extreme necessity, this individual may utilize this rank when the tool above it fails.

For instance, if the employee mentioned earlier fails to perform their tasks creatively and improvisationally, they may attempt to learn and understand the subject matter for a period. However, if they are unable to cope under extreme pressure, they put pressure on themselves and seek help from others. This sudden approach surprises those around them, as this individual is typically distant, independent, and reluctant to seek help or collaborate with others.

This person is not motivated by a desire to collaborate with others and build teamwork, but rather by necessity. Despite trying all other higher-level tools to achieve their primary goal of making money, in some cases, they are compelled to complete a necessary unwanted task. To strengthen this area, it's best to practice using it with aversion until they become accustomed to it, as the lack of use of a muscle weakens it.

Let's recap what we've learned so far about these five engines and the rules for analyzing them:

The five engines function differently depending on their position in the hierarchy, with the higher drives being more consciously acknowledged and impactful in a person's daily life. Conversely, weaker drives tend to be neglected because people are less aware of their influence, which is reflected in their behavior.

The first rank is the basic engine that guides a person's decisions, determining whether to pursue something or not. People always seek to derive some benefit from their actions.

The second rank moderates the first level, creating balance in a person's life. This balance fluctuates in difficult decisions, where people may initially rely on the primary engine, but eventually, the brakes rebounds and restores equilibrium, compensating for any harm caused by neglecting it.

The third rank, known as the comfort zone, represents a natural inclination for individuals to settle into after experiencing success or failure in attaining the goals set by higher ranks. It is during this phase that people often find themselves caught in a state of confusion and uncertainty, pondering whether they should strive for the objectives of the first and second ranks or content themselves with the stability and security offered by this zone.

The fourth and fifth layers are ignored types of energy and considered as tools used to serve the upper levels, only called upon when necessary and with reluctance. The difference between them lies in the degree of urgency required to engage them. Using the fourth engine is relatively easy in times of need, whereas calling upon the fifth engine is much more challenging. Each level serves as a tool for the level above it in the hierarchy, and they are all interconnected.

People differ in the order of these categories, resulting in diverse behaviors towards their goals. Probability theory suggests that there are 120 possible permutations for ranking these five categories, meaning people worldwide can be grouped into 120 similar samples based on their orientations, with each sample differing from the others in some way.

There exists a configuration that inherently bolsters its possessor towards triumph, while conversely, there is a constraining configuration, yet this does not imply that the proprietor is incapable of managing it and emerging victorious.

Let's say there is a person named David, and let his five drives be arranged in the following order:

Ranking	Engine name
Primary engine	Money
Brakes	Knowledge
Comfort zone	Emotions
Main tool	Health
Blind spot	Relationships

Due to his prioritization of financial goals above all else, he is relentlessly pursuing financial freedom. He's a money-minded individual who consistently seeks to amplify his efforts towards achieving wealth. However, as he places his thirst for knowledge in second place, it creates a distraction from his money-oriented mindset and allows him to appreciate education and learning more profoundly. He may be the type of person who struggles to make a decision regarding dropping out of university and launching a business venture similar to that of the prototypical entrepreneur.

At this stage, he is uncertain which option would be more beneficial: attempting to acquire wealth quickly and then pursuing the PhD degree he envisions having later on, or investing time in education and gaining wealth through that path. This contradiction isn't confined to academic learning alone; it extends to all aspects of life and the various projects he takes on.

He grapples with the dilemma of whether he should focus on acquiring knowledge to succeed in his endeavors and make money or prioritize earning money mechanically using any available way without investing in learning, leaving the responsibility of specialized research to his subordinates. Even if he chooses the latter route, given his slight preference for money over education, he can't help but feel unsettled and envious of individuals who possess greater expertise in the topics that intrigue him.

He yearns to have devoted more of his time to learning the things he's passionate about but ultimately opts to leverage the knowledge of others to attain colossal wealth for himself.

The contradiction in his life creates a delicate balance, prompting him to strive for equilibrium between his arduous pursuit of wealth and setting aside time for learning. Should he fail in either endeavor, he finds contentment in the enjoyment of his life. Due to his strong inclination towards maintaining a constant sense of well-being, he tends to exert less effort in learning and working. This preference for feeling good all the time creates obstacles to achieving higher levels of learning and financial success, as he remains content within his current psychological state.

He is content and uninterested in dramatically altering his emotions. Individuals like him may not have grand financial ambitions and instead quickly gravitate towards spirituality, entertainment, or any other sources of comfort. They perceive these pursuits as a form of psychological wealth that cannot be achieved through money or scientific status.

David, in particular, may be cavalier about his health, turning excessively to alcoholic drinks, overindulging in food, and other unhealthy habits to cater to his comfort zone, seeking pleasure and appropriate psychological sensations. Moreover, he will be less socially inclined than most people, preferring introversion and isolation to acquiring new friends or acquaintances.

Let's consider another example. Stefanie's strong inclination to maintain relationships with others suggests a potential tendency towards seeking fame, building connections, and being excessively kind towards strangers. People with such inclinations often spend their entire day engaged in conversations and experience significant discomfort when they are away from social interactions. The presence of health in the second rank acts as a moderating factor, tempering these tendencies.

Ranking	Engine name
Primary engine	Relationships
Brakes	Health
Comfort zone	Money
Main tool	Emotions
Blind spot	Knowledge

Stefanie finds herself in a state of contradiction. Will she attend a party with many friends or will she be compelled to consume sugary foods? What if all the dishes contain meat while she maintains a vegetarian diet? Will she shake hands and exchange pleasantries or are there contagious diseases present? Stefanie's concern for her health will curtail her direct communication and closeness when building relationships with others, particularly those whose healthy habits aren't as evolved as hers.

Money falls within Stefanie's comfort zone, where she finds contentment when in possession of it but experiences significant unease when spending it. This exacerbates the contradiction within her personality. While she desires more friends, she does not spend or invest in them. Instead, she expects others to spend their money to make her feel secure and comfortable. By not venturing beyond this comfort zone, she risks being unsuccessful in her relationships as she desires. Spending, generosity, and investment in her followers will enable her to create the alliance she seeks to lead.

With the emotion engine being used as an emergency tool, Stefanie is unlikely to resort to solving problems based on emotions. She is always interested in her external relationships and the emotions of others. If necessary, she may use this tool to introspect and understand the reasons behind someone's refusal of a relationship or her behavior. It's hard for her to suppress these matters and turn to wishful thinking or spirituality to quiet the inner turmoil, but she is compelled to use this tool in such situations. Since activating knowledge or expertise is difficult for her, she will never prefer to solve her problems using tried-and-tested scientific methods.

When it comes to problems in her relationships, she may find it challenging to turn to spirituality or emotional solutions to suppress and control her feelings. However, she will never feel the urge to seek out solutions online or in specialized books.

Undoubtedly, you have observed the significant differences between David and Stefanie's approaches. Their disparity transcends mere orientations and delves into the depths of their being. Their daily actions are steered by five driving forces, illuminating even the most trivial actions in this context. Consequently, it is possible to discern which of the two individuals is more adept at accomplishing a task.

Considering their long-term aspirations, who do you think would thrive in businesses building ? Would it be David, with his focus on money and learning, or Stefanie, with her emphasis on relationships and safety? David possesses all the qualities of a successful businessman, whereas Stefanie embodies the persona of a social influencer.

When it comes to everyday life, there's no doubt that Stefanie is the type of person who would be more inclined to play energetically on the streets and draw a crowd. Her ambition to captivate and charm people makes her more proficient than David at manipulating and drawing them into her sphere of influence.

As you progress in your reading, you will gain a more in-depth understanding of this analysis. Nonetheless, this summary provides a glimpse into the fundamental disparity between individuals in their behavior, shaped by their varying interests and predispositions. This principle will aid in the classification of individuals into distinct types and open up new avenues for exploration and analysis, which we will delve into in the next chapter.

CHAPTER 4

The Innate Role

"Each man has his own vocation; his talent is his call. There is one direction in which all space is open to him." - Ralph Waldo Emerson

Throughout the preceding chapters, we have explored the five engines that are responsible for shaping individuals' intentions, behaviors, and actions towards their desired objectives. The potency of these engines varies in accordance with their respective order on the scale, thereby resulting in a mosaic of human types. By applying probability theory, we discover that there exist 120 potential sequences for these five engines.

This implies that there are 120 strains of humanity that bear many shared qualities, while also diverging in certain aspects. To simplify our study of these diverse types, we shall employ an additional tool of classification. It is worth noting that there are 24 conceivable outcomes wherein the wealth engine reigns supreme, and likewise with the remaining engines. Hence, we can classify individuals into five broad categories (a consequence of 120 divided by 24), predicated on their primary engine.

The Five Sects

Human beings can be classified into five distinct sects according to their aspirations, innate talents, designated societal roles, and the most basic form of success they seek. This categorization enables us to better understand the diversity among individuals and the unique paths they pursue in their lives. It is important to note, however, that while this classification system provides a framework for analysis, it does not capture the full complexity of human nature.

Entrepreneurs

These are individuals for whom the drive for financial gain is their primary motivator. Money is the lifeblood of their businesses, and they are willing to do whatever it takes to accumulate wealth. Although we use the term "Entrepreneurs" for the sake of simplicity, it should be noted that not all of them are true innovators. Among their types, you will find both the visionary creators of new enterprises and the dedicated employees who help to bring those visions to life.

Sages

The primary driving force for this group is their concern for maintaining good health and staying safe. They share a common commitment to valuing and safeguarding their own well-being. Again, while the term "Sages" is used as an umbrella term, not all members of this group are the same. There are variations in their status, but they all belong to the larger group of individuals who prioritize health.

Spiritualists

These are individuals who are motivated by their emotions and selected feelings. They share a deep respect for the spirit and a desire to nourish it in every way possible. Some turn to religious practices or meditation, while others find spiritual fulfillment through music, entertainment, or travel. Despite their differences, they all devote more time than other groups to nourishing the soul and experiencing the emotions that uplift them.

Scholars

Individuals in this group are motivated by the pursuit of knowledge. The term "Scholars" is used loosely here, as it applies to anyone who values education and devotes significant time to it. There is great variation in their ranks due to the other priorities that drive them. Members of this group excel in various academic and practical fields, making them the most creative and innovative group of individuals when they learn and apply knowledge effectively.

Influencers

The final group, "Influencers," comprises individuals who prioritize relationships and the maintenance of social ties. They share a passion for social interaction, fame, and the ability to influence others, and they are skilled in community building, leadership, politics, and control. While they all have a deep love for connections, their individual methods for forming and maintaining those connections can differ greatly.

The 20 Factions

The five sects we have just enumerated are subdivided into four distinct factions, each with members who share the same first and second engine. Despite their shared allegiance to a given sect, each faction presents a unique profile that distinguishes it from its counterparts. I invite you to peruse the diagram on the next page to glean a comprehensive grasp of the intricate architecture of the entrepreneur sect.

The Factions of The Entrepreneurs Sect

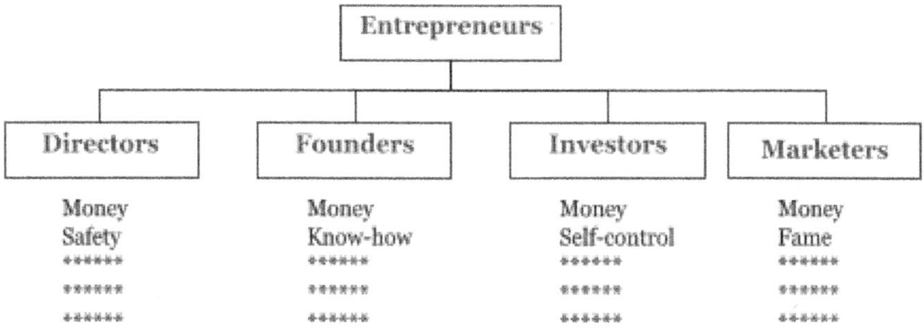

Directors are individuals whose primary driving force is money, placing it in the first rank, followed by health in the second rank. This intense desire for wealth is tempered by a cautious approach to expending their energy, as they do not wish to exhaust themselves or jeopardize their health for the sake of money. They prefer work that yields a high salary without causing undue fatigue or health risks. Members of this faction are characterized by a low energy for work and a propensity for laziness, but this disposition can also make them successful in delegating work to others, making them suitable for roles as directors and coordinators.

They demonstrate creativity in their projects, no matter how simple, as they find optimal ways to earn money without overexerting themselves. However, not everyone in this faction is a director, as some are regular employees or craftsmen, and a person's eligibility for a job does not necessarily translate to their daily life. The aim of this book is to help individuals identify their latent tendencies towards specific goals and how this influences their behavior and decision-making.

The founders represent a group of entrepreneurs in which the acquisition of knowledge takes a secondary role. Their intense desire for wealth is accompanied by a strong thirst for knowledge, often resulting in a conflict between the two. This contradiction, however, enables them to possess a wealth of ideas and information that surpasses that of their peers. Unlike directors who often delegate work to others, the founders concentrate on generating innovative ideas, solving intricate problems, and establishing new companies and institutions based on their acquired knowledge. They possess remarkable creativity and the ability to generate wealth from seemingly nothing.

Investors are a group of individuals who are concerned with both money and emotional control. While the desire for wealth is a strong motivator, they also seek to regulate their emotions, which can inhibit their efforts to earn money. As a result, they often rely on easier methods to make a profit, emphasizing the psychological aspect that they value highly. This duality in motivation creates a unique mentality that is well-suited to the concept of the artisan investor, who regards emotions as an essential factor in their profit or loss.

Meanwhile, **marketers** seek both money and social status, often pursuing roles that allow them to combine the two, such as content creation. This doesn't necessarily mean that all members of the faction follow this approach, but they excel at promoting their own ideas or those of others.

You may have noticed our analytical approach by now. The labels we use for each group or faction are not as important as understanding the interests that arise due to the ordering of engines, the analysis method employed, and the ability to identify appropriate tasks based on the nature of each group's members. While I have chosen a label that I find appropriate, it doesn't mean that you don't have the freedom to label these variables as you see fit.

The Factions of The Sages Sect

The primary driving force for the sage sect is their concern for maintaining good health. They share a common commitment to valuing and safeguarding their own well-being. Again, while the term "sage sect" is used as an umbrella term, not all members of this group are the same. There are variations in their status, but they all belong to the larger group of individuals who prioritize health.

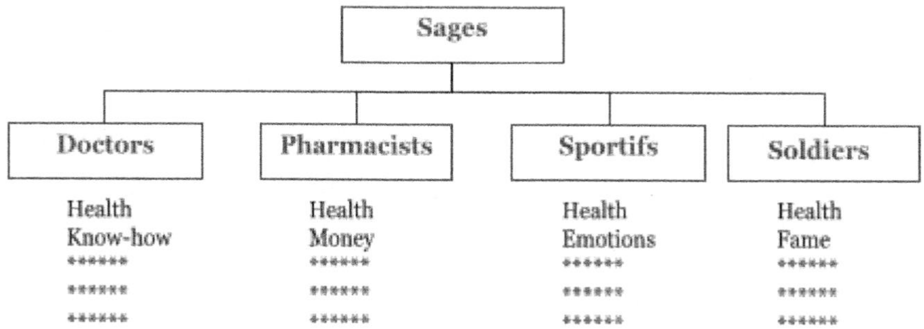

The faction of **doctors** is composed of individuals who prioritize overall health and simultaneously strive to acquire a diverse range of skills. This enables them to learn about various aspects related to nutrition, fitness, biology, medicine, and general well-being, regardless of their professional background. With a comprehensive understanding in this field, they aim to incorporate this knowledge into their daily lives for personal wellness or to assist others in achieving optimal health. You can easily recognize them because they are always eager to give you health advice and share medical or nutrition information that you may not have heard before.

Laboratory technicians or **pharmacists** are a group of individuals who prioritize health, but they also have a strong desire to earn money. There is nothing wrong with valuing money, and we are not trying to downplay its importance in this book. Their drive to earn money while helping others attain good health motivates them to work diligently in producing various health-related products, such as medicines, herbal mixtures, foods, nutrition plans, and anything else that can benefit people's health and generate income for them.

There is a contrast between this group and the doctor faction. The latter focuses on finding a scientific solution to medical problems and does not mind profiting from it. Conversely, the pharmacist faction seeks to transform the solution into a product and sell it. It is highly likely that the owners of pharmaceutical and vaccine manufacturing companies, who have chosen these industries based on their conviction, belong to this faction. Please note that the categorization does not imply that members of this faction are necessarily working in the field of pharmacy. However, if they choose to, they may have a better chance of achieving important breakthroughs compared to those who have less inherent interest in finding a cure. You may have come across some of them in your neighborhood, including individuals who are illiterate but still have a strong desire to help. I had a neighbor like this who always tried to assist me by providing herbs during the winter or attempting to sell me various items over time. And believe me, she has gained confidence over time and now attracts clients from all over the country who come to try her effective mixtures.

The sportifs are more concerned with physical and mental health than others. They prefer to maintain their physical health directly because they believe it affects their mental state. This contradiction drives them to seek out healthy and enjoyable activities at the same time, making them more inclined to activities that have this nature, such as sports, for example, which is why we have chosen to call them by this name. Members of this faction differ in their other underlying motives that drive them to engage in the activities they choose.

Soldiers are a collective of individuals who not only prioritize their own well-being but also place value on those in their vicinity. They aspire to establish relationships, attain fame, achieve social status, and surround themselves with loved ones. This equilibrium creates an impression of individuals who are genuinely concerned about the health and safety of others, focusing on defending it rather than instructing others, as the doctor faction does. Their distinguishing traits encompass a pronounced inclination towards sacrifice, heroic deeds, and safeguarding life, the physical body, and everything associated with it.

The Factions of The Spiritualists Sect

The name "Spiritualists" may not be inclusive of all members around them, but we chose it only to express the desire of these individuals to nurture the spirit and evoke emotions more than other sects. You can always use the name you prefer as long as you understand the meaning behind it. The Spiritualists, in turn, are divided into multiple factions according to the driving force that restrains their main engine.

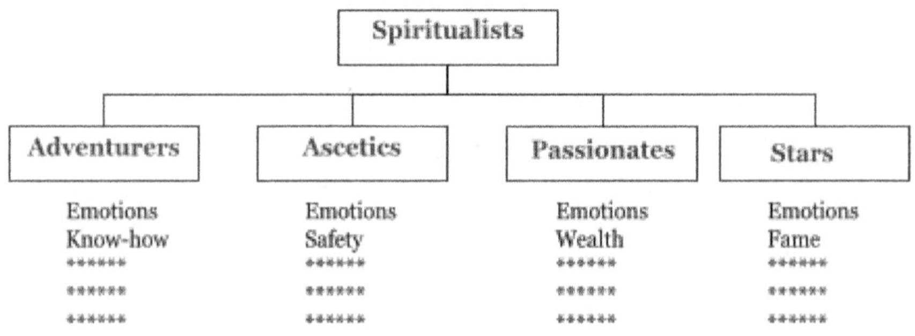

Adventurers are people who are primarily interested in experiencing spiritual and psychological pleasure through various emotions and sensations. They also have a strong desire to learn and uncover mysteries. This contradiction in their desires makes them strive to make learning enjoyable. They choose to acquire knowledge and skills that evoke new feelings in them. Adventurers enjoy trying new things every day and strive to learn from these experiences and understand their meanings. They are characterized by their boundless energy and intense desire for travel, exploration, search, and discovery of adrenaline and dopamine-inducing experiences.

Ascetics are a group of people who prioritize their spiritual well-being over their physical health. They seek positive emotions and strive for an inner sense of happiness, free from the complexities of external pleasures. However, they approach progress and expending energy with caution and restraint because they care about maintaining their health.

Their primary motivation is to nourish and enjoy their soul, but they avoid indulging in pleasures that may harm their health, such as drinking alcohol or seeking unsafe thrills in any activity. Their approach is to abstain from pleasures for extended periods and occasionally indulge in them, or they opt for activities and practices that bring them joy without compromising their health, such as prayer, meditation, and spiritual living. Therefore, the term "ascetic" can accurately describe this true monk or devotee personality.

Stars are individuals who are primarily interested in experiencing positive emotions and sensations, as well as forming good relationships with others and gaining recognition and fame among them. This makes them potential candidates for stardom and fame. Their desire to experience positive feelings leads them to choose enjoyable activities such as music, art, or sports, while their drive to build social status motivates them to work hard to gain fame and establish a good reputation. Stars excel in fields such as singing, acting, or any area where they can enjoy themselves and express their feelings to others.

Passionates, unlike stars, are not concerned with social status but with accumulating more money every day. They seek to experience all that is beautiful, but they are also willing to put in the effort and suffer a little to achieve financial freedom. This contradiction between the desire to feel positive and the willingness to endure hardship, difficulty, and financial risks drives them to choose the best tasks that combine the two, and this is true creativity.

Passionates produce many artistic works, compositions, or any creative expressions for humanity, but their desire is usually not for fame but for accumulating wealth, even if it means not appearing in public. Passionates often work in secrecy and avoid appearing as long as they earn money from what they do, making them work as composers, authors or film directors, where their direct appearance does not matter as it does with stars.

The Factions of The Scholars Sect

Scholars share a commonality in their reverence for knowledge and their ability to dedicate significant amounts of time to learning, as compared to other members of society. However, this similarity does not make them identical; they also differ in their inclinations and even in the energy that restrains their desire to learn.

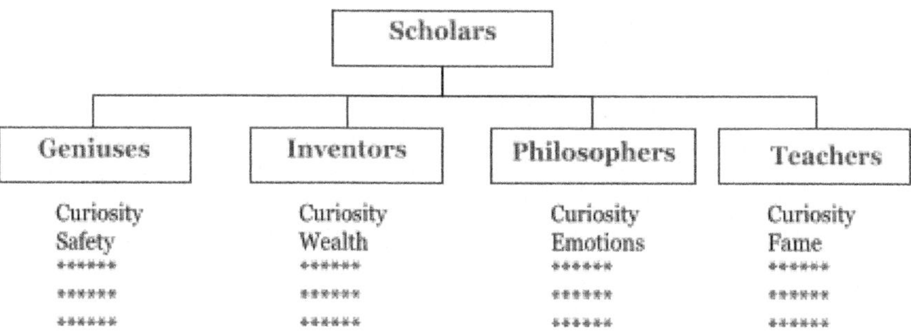

Geniuses are a group of individuals who aspire to learn a lot of things, but their learning energy is low. They are characterized by laziness, love of sleep, and a reduction in movement, unless it is stimulating for them. They cannot work in fields that require physical effort. This contradiction in their lives drives them to learn in small amounts every day and to choose only the necessary information, as their energy depletes quickly. Continuing in this way makes them learn the basics of everything, they try to adjust the information they obtain, deduce what they do not know or what they need. They try to understand the big picture and hidden ideas and do not care much about details, and this is precisely the definition of a genius, as they do not need to study everything in depth to understand it, but rather connect simple daily ideas they learn, trying to understand the big picture.

They have the ability to grasp intricate concepts and deconstruct systems into simpler, manageable parts. Although they don't have a lot of energy to turn their knowledge into reality, they are primarily interested in comprehending things to avoid encountering complicated issues in the future.

Inventors are people who are passionate about uncovering the mysteries of the universe and solving problems that not only affect themselves, but also humanity as a whole. However, they are also motivated by financial rewards for their work. This creates a contradiction that drives them to pursue fields that are in demand, rather than those they are personally interested in. To them, knowledge is a commodity that is subject to supply and demand, and they must compete to stay up-to-date with the latest technologies in order to turn a profit.

When you think of inventors, figures like Elon Musk might come to mind, and for good reason. Musk chooses to focus on areas that require competition and expertise in fields like artificial intelligence and space exploration, rather than pursuing his personal interests. Inventors are known for their ability to develop innovative systems and utilize the latest scientific discoveries to advance humanity, rather than simply focusing on information that is of little practical use.

Philosophers are interested in exploring abstract ideas related to human existence, such as happiness, pain, the human psyche, and all aspects of humanity and its destiny. They are known for their sharpness of thought and their ability to argue and change people's perspectives on various topics. Additionally, many of them are talented writers, artists, and creatives, including well-known musicians, deep thinkers, and filmmakers.

Their orientations and skills stem from their inherent curiosity, drive to explore deeper meanings, and ability to evoke positive emotions. The inherent contradiction between their thirst for knowledge and their need for emotional fulfillment compels them to seek solutions and explanations regarding the meaning of life. Sometimes, the ideas they share with others may only be fragments of what is going on in their minds, and they may struggle to explain them to others. However, these individuals often develop their abilities to express their thoughts and ideas more effectively through improving their social communication skills and building stronger relationships with others.

Teachers possess a broad range of knowledge and exhibit a desire for recognition and esteem, a result of their intellectual prowess. The acquisition of social ties and status take a back seat to their thirst for knowledge. These individuals are characterized by their eagerness to share their knowledge with a wide audience, highlighting its abundance and quality. This fuels their motivation to continue learning and search for novel methods of conveying their insights to others, thus encapsulating the true essence of a genuine educator.

The Factions of The Influencers Sect

Influencers possess comparable communication skills and possess the ability to maintain harmonious relationships and consistency among individuals. They possess an unwavering eagerness to create numerous relationships on a vast scale, command influence and control, or simply gain the respect of others. Like many others, they can be classified into four factions depending on the driving force that hinders their efforts to establish swift connections with others.

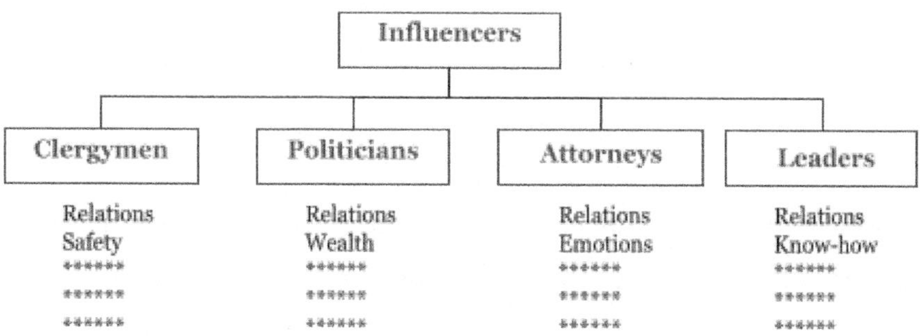

Politicians exhibit a paradoxical nature in their aspirations, oscillating between seeking fame, exerting influence over people, building and governing communities, on one hand, and striving to accumulate wealth and material success, on the other. This dichotomy situates members of this faction at the forefront of diplomacy, endowed with the art of manipulating language and exploiting others' skills to achieve glory without harming. They yearn to control people and preserve their positive and respectable image, thereby diverting attention from their shortcomings. Simultaneously, they endeavor to attain their financial goals.

These individuals possess an innate talent for swaying opinions and diffusing conflicts. Although they need not be seasoned politicians, they often occupy positions of influence in various domains, from small to big corporations and institutions. Their unrelenting drive to forge connections and manipulate their peers is often misconstrued as deceitfulness or opportunism, but in truth, their ultimate goal is to affect sweeping reforms in the lives of others. These astute operators possess an unwavering confidence in their ability to solve complex societal problems, and are unapologetic about demanding fair remuneration for their services.

As with all members of the influencer group, **attorneys** are known for their ability to resolve conflicts and exert their opinions on others or influence them directly or indirectly. However, they stand apart from other factions because of their low-key approach. They don't typically expend a great deal of effort, as they believe that wise words, advice, or guiding laws are sufficient to effect change. Attorneys prioritize the health and safety of others, which leads them to dedicate their lives to protecting and guiding others toward what is beneficial and away from harm. Above all, they desire for people to live in harmony, to respect laws, and to heed the advice and judgments they offer in order to effect change and safeguard themselves from destruction.

Leaders stand out among other groups for their wisdom and extensive knowledge, which gives them a far-reaching perspective on the future of humanity and the direction it's headed. They leverage this insight to guide and unite others, leaving an indelible mark on society. In contrast to politicians who rely on diplomatic language, leaders are candid and direct in their speech, driven by the goal of establishing strong and meaningful relationships rather than manipulating others' emotions to achieve their ends.

Clergymen, on the other hand, are known for their intense desire to forge connections with others while also preserving their spirituality and savoring all the positive emotions and sensations that life has to offer. They are compassionate and empathetic, always ready to sacrifice themselves for the greater good. Despite being highly social beings, they often spend much of their time in solitude, engaging in activities that nourish their souls, such as worship, music, or other forms of spiritual expression. Ultimately, their true purpose lies in setting a positive example for others in handling difficult emotions and using spirituality as a means of finding peace and solace.

The Impact of the Remaining Ranks

Although the first and second levels are readily noticeable to users, they often begin to pay less attention to them over time. As the saying goes, "too much of a good thing can be harmful." For example, an individual's obsession with money may initially drive them, but eventually, it becomes ingrained in their nature. If asked about their desires, they may not even mention money, despite it being their primary motivator, and instead focus on something of lesser significance, as the pursuit of money has become automatic for them.

This is precisely what occurs with the third layer, known as the comfort zone. Despite having less impact than the first and second engines in reality, it is the most coveted layer among users. The comfort zone significantly influences an individual's tendencies and decisions, often resulting in behavior that differs from their group's overall behavior. Consequently, this opens up the possibility of further classification, with each faction branching out into groups based on the prevailing driving force within their third layer.

Let's take an example to avoid getting too complex. Take the faction of investors, each member holding the following ranking:

1. Money
2. Emotions
3. *********
4. *********
5. *********

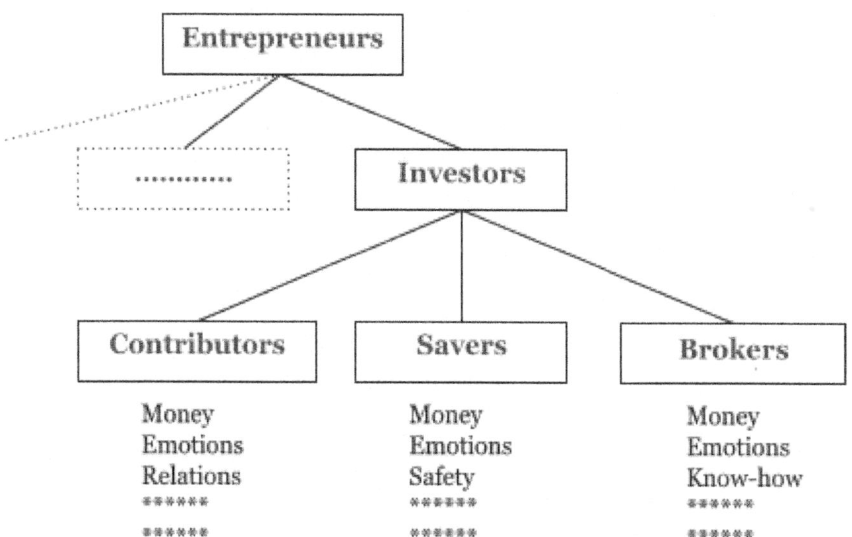

The third layer is the reason why factions tend to divide into groups, as the field of investing and its methods vary depending on the user's preferences for investment tools and the areas they naturally gravitate towards. Brokers, or whatever label we choose for classification, strive to understand the nuances of investing and how to build an investment system that suits them, relying on knowledge and strategy rather than just gambling and emotional management.

Contributors are a unique type of investors, as they bring a human element to their investment approach. Their desire to earn money and manage their emotions is coupled with an emphasis on leveraging their relationships and investing in the human element in others. Maintaining a good reputation and status is important to them, as their relationships are built on a sensitive foundation. Contributors invest in relationships and see building a network of followers, allies, or customers as the best type of investment. Consequently, they strive to demonstrate that their investments and financial sacrifices benefit society, even if they also bring individual profits to themselves.

Savers want to expend less energy and minimize risk because they care about their long-term psychological, mental, and physical safety, and they believe that saving with a small interest rate is better than risky investments.

It's possible to further analyze and delve into an individual's inclinations, which can clarify the bigger picture and reveal the reasons behind people's differences in tendencies. However, I won't delve into categorizing all the types in this book, and I may even produce a separate book entitled "120 Personalities" to explore the differences among these characters. What's important now is to grasp the idea in a general sense and recognize your innate role. You can now practice this on your own by assigning numerous labels to different types of people based on their differences in the third and even fourth ranks.

Specials Combinations

Twins are individuals who share the same order of the five engines, which makes them completely identical. They are capable of working together as partners to achieve common goals. The bond between twins is unique, as they share a deep connection that is beyond comprehension. The similarities between them are not just limited to their goals, but they also share a remarkable level of emotional and mental connection.

Opposites are individuals whose engine orders are completely reversed from each other. They speak a different language regarding their goals and ways of achieving them, which makes it difficult for them to understand each other. However, they can complement each other in certain situations. Opposites can provide unique perspectives and approaches to a problem that may not have been considered otherwise.

They can learn from each other's differences, and their collaboration can lead to innovative solutions.

Partners are individuals who have subtle differences between them, typically in the first or the second engines. They are similar in many ways, but each person has unique strengths that complement the other's weaknesses. Partners understand and respect each other's differences, and they work together to achieve a shared goal. When they collaborate, they bring out the best in each other, and their collective efforts lead to great success.

Sometimes, random arrangements can create unexpected harmony when approached in a dual way. There are no rules for this yet, as it needs to be studied and analyzed statistically. Nevertheless, it is a self-evident fact that differences present an opportunity for integration. Artists consider yellow and blue as complementary colors, which is a testament to how different elements can blend seamlessly to create a beautiful whole. This principle applies to life as well, where people can complement each other's strengths and weaknesses to achieve greater success together.

Why Bother with Similar Possibilities?

The resemblance of these personalities does not imply that they are indistinguishable. A minor variation in mathematics denotes that A does not equal B. One may assume that merely a difference in order does not influence the conduct of an individual, particularly the variance between the fourth and fifth rank. However, this becomes apparent in practical life, particularly when it occurs unconsciously in the individual.

If, for instance, you unconsciously prioritize knowledge over relationships, and these engines occupy the lower ranks of the scale, you may resort to making dissimilar decisions from those who prioritize relationships when it becomes necessary. This may result, for example, in your application of a plan that you learned in childhood or from your parents, while those who value relationships consult others and rely on the opinions of many who say the same thing.

These straightforward decisions modify the trajectory of an individual's life and establish whether they are moving towards success or ruination. Therefore, we must harness this power to our benefit by being mindful of it, rather than allowing it to control us and determine our present and future selves.

The 120 Personalities Summarized

1. There are many criteria that can be used to classify people, including the five hidden drivers that urge them to focus on certain goals, orientations, decisions, and behaviors.
2. There are 120 possible arrangements of the five engines, which can be classified into five broad categories based on differences in the first rank.
3. Individuals in the same sect share the long-term overarching goal in essence, despite differences in goals articulation.
4. Each sect can be further divided into four factions based on differences in the second rank, resulting in 20 factions in total.
5. Members of the same faction share the long-term overarching goal, innate abilities and talents, as well as common direct obstacles. However, each faction differs from the others, even if they belong to the same.
6. Each faction is divided into three groups that share the same abilities and talents but differ from each other within the same faction in their conscious declared desires, behaviors, and orientations.
7. Each group is further divided into twins, who only differ in the two last ranks, with the difference lying in the safe haven they turn to in times of need and aversion.
8. Twins are individuals who hold the same rank and are soul partners when it comes to goals.

9. Incompatible arrangements may lead to aversion and conflicting interests, and it is important for one to know the group to which someone belongs if their goals require working with others, so they do not get frustrated in achieving their objectives.
10. The groups, sub-teams, and categories can be named anything, as naming does not usually reflect the content.
11. The better one understands how their personal drivers influence them, the more they can control their objectives and overcome obstacles.
12. Choosing real goals that suit a person depends on their understanding of the categories, groups, sub-teams, weaknesses, strengths, and good self-awareness.
13. Choosing the right goal may require dealing with it in a purely arithmetic manner to achieve success.

CHAPTER 5

Abilities Assessment

Once you have identified your desires, it becomes crucial to recognize your abilities. In fact, your scale of goals serves as an indicator of your talents and capabilities. If your top-ranking engine is money, it signifies that you belong to the league of entrepreneurs and possess a strong aptitude for achieving success in a venture and persevering until its completion. However, if you're not aware of this fact, you won't effectively harness this potential to attain your desired outcome.

To better understand, let's recall the unique traits associated with each engine, determined by its place on the five-step scale of goals. Skills occupy the first and second positions on the scale, whereas obstacles and weaknesses reside in the fourth and fifth positions. The third position remains neutral, capable of either contributing to one's success if effectively managed or becoming an obstacle that leads to failure.

Money Engine Effects

As a primary engine, this vehicle of success aims to inspire its owner to complete tasks and reap financial rewards. That's why entrepreneurs possess an intense work ethic, demonstrate patience when finishing projects, exhibit ambition and dedication, take calculated and daring risks, and possess a strong desire to achieve substantial wealth. Those who have this engine in such a position are well-suited to become millionaires or even billionaires.

Strengths as a primary engine:

- Patience
- Dedicated and energetic approach to work
- Perseverance
- Ambition and willpower
- Willingness to risk
- Chasing opportunities
- Tenacity
- Belief that it will work, whatever happens
- Pragmatism
- Decisiveness

When money is in the brakes mode, it assumes a defensive role. Individuals who have the money engine ranked second exhibit financial wisdom, possess strong analytical skills, approach money-making with careful planning, harbor a keen desire to preserve and expand their wealth, and are capable of undertaking projects, albeit to a lesser extent than entrepreneurs. Those who possess this configuration can readily attain financial freedom.

Strengths as brakes:

- Calculative personality
- Self-control
- Natural ability for strategic planning to minimize financial loss
- Anticipating the future
- Taking calculated risks
- Considering worst-case scenarios
- Being realistic in projects (less ambitious)
- Practicing wise budgeting naturally

As a comfort zone, money strives to make its owner stingy and fearful of losing it. It often leads to limited financial intelligence, which arises when attempting to earn money and seeking easy methods for doing so. Those who possess this engine in this zone prefer to save securely and minimize the risks associated with financial ventures.

Strengths & Weaknesses within the comfort zone:

- Fear of losing
- Frugality
- Pessimistic tendencies
- Greed and desire for excessive wealth
- Fantasizing about money
- Unstable work rhythm
- Balanced Consumer vs Producer mindset

It's important to note that these aspects can be both strengths and weaknesses, and their application is dependent on the user. The comfort zone plays a crucial role in determining success or failure. It often hinders the utilization of one's primary and secondary engines.

at the 4th rank, money is no longer motivating, and thus, higher ranks in the scale surpass this engine. The owner of this position is unable to sustain projects and becomes a consumer rather than a producer.

Weaknesses within the 4th rank :

- Impatience
- Lack of dedication and low energy in approaching work
- Giving up easily
- Lack of ambition and willpower
- Avoidance of any risk or potential embarrassment
- Ignoring or not pursuing opportunities
- Lack of tenacity or persistence
- Doubt and lack of belief in success
- Idealism or impracticality
- Indecisiveness or hesitancy

At the fifth rank, the influence of the money engine compels the user to adopt a consumer mindset and makes them highly susceptible to financial deception. This vulnerability arises from a lack of financial knowledge and a tendency to acquire possessions without considering future planning to break free from this cycle. If the owner of this position fails to learn how to acquire wealth by utilizing the other ranks, it can potentially lead to poverty.

Weaknesses within the 5th rank :

- Impulsive personality.
- Lack of self-control.
- Difficulty in strategic planning.
- Less financial knowledge or lack of skills in minimizing losses & poor budgeting practices.
- Difficulty in anticipating the future.
- Taking reckless risks, such as gambling.
- Neglecting worst-case scenarios.
- Being overly optimistic.

Safety Engine Effects

When health is the primary driving force, users typically possess the following strengths, as it operates in an assertive mode:

- Prioritizing self-care.
- Wisdom.
- Discipline and commitment.
- Insight.
- Carefulness
- Energy, youth and vitality
- Resilience
- Risk analysis
- Empathy towards others' health

When health adopts a defensive stance, users still exhibit strengths that manifest in the following forms:

- Paying attention to details
- Proactive approach
- Mindfulness and concentration skills.
- Excessive concern about one's health
- Good Stress management
- Moderate energy to use the body
- Defensive pessimism
- Caution
- Foresight in predicting risks

The health engine, when operating within a comfort zone, tends to influence its user to embrace a lazy and low-energy lifestyle. They may hastily consume products or adopt health practices without thorough examination, easily convinced of their benefits. However, if the user fails to harness the potential benefits of this comfort zone, they may find themselves succumbing to its weaknesses.

- A propensity for relaxation
- Hesitancy to engage in activities until their safety is ensured
- Laziness
- Trusting information based on its benefit, not accuracy

Weaknesses within the 4th rank:

- Neglecting self-care.
- Rashness
- Indiscipline.
- Ignorance.
- Carelessness.
- Constant fatigue.
- Fragility.
- Impulsiveness.
- Apathy.

In this position, the owner of this engine tends to be impulsive and indifferent to their health, lacking focus on the consequences of their actions, and more interested in pursuing pleasures.

At the fifth rank, individuals begin to disregard their body's signals and consequently suffer adverse consequences. They may experience exhaustion, fatigue, and frequent illnesses due to their neglect of physical health.

Weaknesses within the 5th rank:

- Inattentiveness or carelessness regarding details.
- Being easily distracted or lacking focus.
- Neglecting or overlooking body safety.
- Inadequate stress management or experiencing high stress levels.
- Low energy levels or a lack of vitality.
- Excessive optimism or an unrealistic positive outlook.
- Displaying recklessness or a lack of caution.
- Restlessness or difficulty in finding relaxation.
- Acting impulsively
- Failing to foresee or assess risks efficiently .

Have you noticed the contrasting nature between the 4th layer and the 1st, as well as the reciprocal characteristics between the 5th and 2nd ranks? This is a result of the inherent symmetry of strengths and weaknesses within the system.

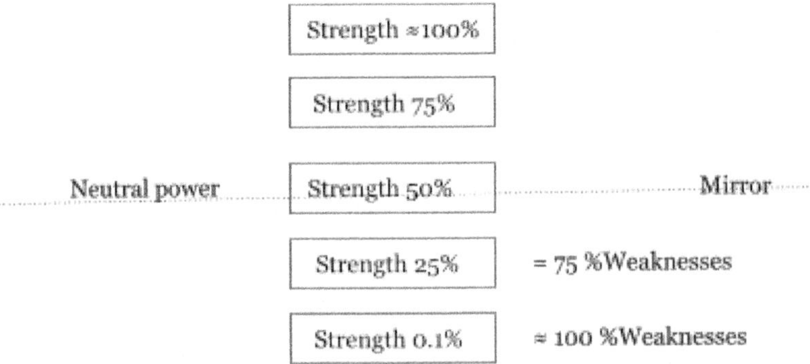

If you know your strengths, you can deduce your weaknesses. You just need to reverse the upper ranks as if there were a mirror in the middle of the comfort zone. Always remember that an engine has the potential to both motivate you when it is your main intention and bring about ruin if you fail to harness the remaining energy it offers. We refer to the 4th layer as a tool, as it is typically utilized in urgent situations. Only in extreme circumstances can you truly leverage the 5th layer and transform weaknesses into strengths.

Emotions Engine Effects

Spiritualist seek all positive emotions, including happiness, and therefore possess the following reflected skills:

- The ability to control emotions.
- The ability to think positively.
- The ability to attract positive emotions such as ambition, willpower, and more.

To explore further, imagine what a hero who possesses mastery over the power of emotion would be like. What skills would they possess? What natural characteristics would they develop over time, starting from childhood? Asking these questions will assist you in compiling a comprehensive list of the potential skills that the emotion engine or any other engine would influence within the system when operating at this layer.

At the 2nd rank, known as the defensive state, users exhibit the following skills:

- Resisting and suppressing negative emotions.
- Maintaining emotional composure.
- The ability to understand their momentary feelings.

To Continue further, envision what a defender of the "Emotion" type would resemble. What would they protect, and what defensive skills would they need to adopt to align with this role?

As a comfort zone, the emotions engine aims to keep its owner oblivious, instinctual, focused on the present, unconcerned about the future, and hesitant to confront or experience negative emotions. To determine the strengths and weaknesses that the user would possess, imagine a hesitant but skilled beginner. How would they appear? how would they repress or demonstrate their skills? Enumerate all the potential skills and weaknesses, which are typically diminished versions of the skills and weaknesses found in the 1st and 2nd ranks.

When attempting to identify the weaknesses triggered by the emotion engine at the 4th rank, consider reversing those that were envisioned at the 1st rank.

For example :

- They struggle with suppressing and disregarding positive emotions.
- They exhibit sudden impulsiveness.
- They lack the ability to control their emotions and let them dictate their actions.

Lastly, apply the same approach to the 2nd and 5th layers:

- Difficulty in reasoning.
- Lack of self-awareness regarding their own emotions.
- Frequently misunderstood or erroneously labeled as cruel.

Continue in a similar manner for the remaining weaknesses.

Knowledge Engine Effects

Scholars pursue all the knowledge that makes them feel intelligent:

- A strong inclination and determination to learn.
- Ability to grasp intricate concepts.
- They decompose any system to understand it in details
- Embracing any challenge as a valuable learning opportunity, irrespective of its practicality.

Individuals who have this engine in a defensive state possess the following skills:

- They selectively learn what is beneficial.
- They strive to simplify and avoid complexity.
- They focus only on the general idea of the subject.

If these individuals utilize the strong side of their comfort zone , they would be confident in their knowledge and possess the following skills:

- Self-confidence
- The ability to argue and defend their opinions
- Promptitude

However, if they misuse the comfort zone, they suffer from:

- Arrogance
- Stubbornness
- Misinformation

Users may have the following weaknesses if the knowledge engine operate as an emergency tool (4th rank):

- Reluctance to learn.
- Settling for simplistic information regardless of its accuracy.
- Lack of knowledge with awareness of their own ignorance (simple ignorance).

And these weaknesses if the engine is innately ignored in the background (5th rank):

- Compound ignorance: They don't know, and they are unaware that they don't know.
- They are easily deceived.
- If no efforts are made, their level of stupidity can easily accumulate.

Relations Engine Effects

Influencers explore all relationships that make them feel valued, leading to the development of innate skills, including:

- The ability to influence people and win their affection.
- Good interpersonal skills.
- The ability to prove themselves.
- The ability to build loyal followers

Individuals who possess this engine in a defensive state exhibit the following skills:

- Ease of reputation maintenance.
- Skill in preserving relationships.
- The skill of advocating for rights.

These relation engine users at the comfort zone mode are self-sufficient in terms of relationships and strike a balance between introversion and extroversion. If they utilize the strong aspect of this area, they possess the following skills:

- Listening to others
- Awareness of their boundaries.
- Balanced introversion and extraversion tendencies

If they misuse the comfort zone aspect, they may experience:

- Critical personality
- Fear of solitude and/or fear of interaction with others
- Weirdness

At the fourth rank, weaknesses start really to affect the user behavior, which can be reflected as :

- Low emotional intelligence
- Less confidence in relations
- Harming others feelings unconsciously

If the relation engine is a blind spot, they would experience complete isolation and struggle in their relationships with others, potentially developing feelings of hostility if they are unable to improve in this area.

- Introversion (non-beneficial type)
- Lack of tact
- Bluntness

Once you have a clear understanding of your personal goal hierarchy, take the time to jot down your strengths and weaknesses on paper, using the information we have provided. Take a closer look at each level and assess how it affects you personally. It's important to validate these findings in real-life situations by reflecting on your behavior and seeking feedback from others. Keep in mind that the arrangement of these engines in a specific order plays a significant role in shaping your character and provides valuable insights into your inherent abilities and shortcomings. It is also up to you to imagine what each of your engines has as strengths or weaknesses, since what we have given is general and not specific to everyone. You have the right to analyze by yourself and build your own ability assessment criteria.

My strengths	My weaknesses
1.	1. ....
2.	2. ....
3.	3. ....
4.	4. ....
5.	5. ....
6.	6. ....
7.	7. ....
8.	8. ....
9.	9. ....
10.	10. ....
11.	11. ....
12.	12. ....
13.	13. ....
14.	14. ....
15.	15. ....
16.	16. ....
17.	17. ....
18.	18. ....
19.	19. ....
20.	20. ....

All you need to do is review your goals and ensure they align with your abilities and talents. This will help you align your desires with your capabilities. We strongly advise against pursuing specific goals solely because you want them and believe you can achieve them, even if they go against your natural abilities. Likewise, we don't recommend abandoning your goals completely just because you possess other talents and abilities. In the next chapter, we will guide you on how to carefully select goals that resonate with your true desires and leverage your innate abilities, so you don't waste valuable time on self-discovery.

Ultimately, our goal is for you to achieve genuine success, which we define as finding balance in your life. To achieve this, it's important to focus on your strengths to accomplish meaningful objectives, even if they weren't initially your top priorities, as they will contribute to attaining what truly matters to you. It's unwise to rely on your weaknesses and flaws to achieve your desires. Instead, your plan should be well-thought-out and based on good goal engineering principles.

Chapter 6

Failure Debugging

One of the main reasons we fail to achieve certain goals is that we often set our sights on objectives that are not in line with our abilities and interests. It's human nature to find it difficult to accept our limitations. However, it's important to note that our intention in this chapter is not to discourage individuals from pursuing their passions. Rather, we seek to distinguish between desire and willpower. Willpower arises from the conviction that you possess the ability to accomplish something, whereas desire stems from a sense of wishful thinking, competition, and a desire to appear successful.

It is crucial that we approach goal-setting in a rational and realistic manner, as striving for goals that are not aligned with our capabilities can result in repeated failure and ultimately hinder us from achieving our true aspirations. This is because, over time, we may become accustomed to failure and lose the motivation to try again.

It is commonly attributed to Einstein that he once said, "Everyone is a genius. But if you judge a fish by its ability to climb a tree, it will live its whole life believing that it is stupid." While we cannot be certain that Einstein actually uttered these words, they nonetheless convey an indisputable truth.

Educational systems established by governments have attempted to equalize students by teaching them the same subjects and testing them in the same areas, despite their differences. This approach has led some individuals to believe that they are failures because they do not excel in certain subjects or because they are not intelligent enough. However, this notion is untrue. Each one of us possesses the potential to succeed and is equipped with the same level of capability, albeit in different forms. Just as every color is indispensable in painting a picture, so too is every individual's unique potential required for achieving success.

Having numerous desires, wishes, and dreams is undoubtedly beneficial, but it is crucial for individuals to prioritize them with rationality and comprehension. The truth is, we can all attain success if we adhere to the innate goals that define us. Success can be envisioned as a specific town on a map, enclosed by several borders. To enter this town, one must locate the nearest gateway in their neighboring town or chart a direct course originating from their own town. The alternative of scouring all the nations of the world in pursuit of the town that purports to be the primary starting point is neither practical nor efficient.

Consider someone who has set their goal priorities in the following order:

1. Money
2. Relationships
3. Health
4. Emotions
5. Knowledge

It is anticipated that an individual of this nature, whether they have experienced failure or possess lesser motivation, would eventually prioritize their health extensively. It serves as a source of comfort for them. While they aspire to achieve financial success, maintain positive relationships with everyone, cultivate a good reputation, and leave a lasting legacy, their actual unpronounced goal would be to find rest for their body, alleviate all fatigue, and steer clear of harm.

But what if this person adopted a misguided approach to achieving success? What if they decided to become a doctor solely to safeguard their health and care for their body? What if they made this decision because they heard in childhood that being a doctor is an honorable profession that helps them understand their body and protect others? Would such a person have the same opportunities for success in this field as someone who possessed the following engines order:

1. Health
2. Knowledge
3. Relationships
4. Emotions
5. Money

Clearly, the latter code reflects the true personality of a successful doctor, as they have an innate desire to protect themselves, acquire knowledge, and cultivate strong relationships with others. In essence, they possess all the qualities necessary for success in the field of medicine.

Let's say that both of them pursued a medical degree based on ignorance and lack of awareness, as society deems it the noblest profession, and children are often taught this from a young age. Despite this, both students are determined to obtain their diplomas, no matter what the cost. Who do you think will excel in their studies? Who do you think will enjoy the profession they're studying and learn with passion? Who will dedicate their life to becoming an outstanding physician who heals people?

It's evident that the second student will have a greater chance of success in this field since they focus on learning and health, which are natural traits of their personality. Conversely, the first student is driven by fear alone, feeling compelled to pursue medicine.

This individual will be surprised by their failure in studies since they don't have the same mastery of the learning process as the second student. Even if the first student graduates with flying colors, they won't become an excellent doctor since they ignored their personal code of success and chose a path that doesn't suit them. They won't be able to commit themselves entirely to this profession because their desire for money and fame will eventually take over, and they'll realize that they've become aware of their abilities only after wasting precious time.

Have you ever noticed how certain individuals seem to have a natural inclination towards success in certain fields? It's not to say that some people are inherently destined to succeed or fail, as everyone has a predisposition towards success, but with different concepts and approaches.

Even if the second code holder were to pursue fame by choosing to be an actor and utilizing their intelligence to master arts, they would ultimately fail. While there are a few fish that can fly, they remain exceptions among the vast majority of marine creatures, and they can never compare to birds. The aquatic nature of these fish ultimately triumphs, and they return to their swimming ways.

Upon gaining awareness, the actor will come to recognize their true passions and develop an intense desire to learn about biology or a related field. This fake actor will persist in his pursuit of success, but he will not hide his true nature from his companions.

He may engage in conversation during lunch, attempting to explain the benefits and drawbacks of certain foods or herbs. He is referred to as "the doctor" by their friends, which leaves them feeling uncomfortable. In the end, he will hear a voice calling from within, reminding them that their true place is in the hospital, not on stage.

We all make mistakes, except for the lucky few who have found a career that aligns with their personality. Children often don't know what they want and are influenced by external factors, which can delay their success until adulthood. It's important for parents to understand their own success codes and then understand their children's codes, in order to guide them towards a smooth path to success rather than imposing their own personalities or values onto their children.

The first step towards success is self-awareness, which involves understanding your natural abilities and talents, as well as your motivations for pursuing a goal. Are you pursuing something because you truly want it, or because it's what everyone else is doing? Once you have this level of self-awareness, you'll be able to enjoy the journey towards success, even if you don't ultimately achieve your original goal. You may even surprise yourself with how much you're capable of achieving, regardless of your age.

Success isn't limited to a particular age range - anyone under sixty is still capable of achieving their goals, and even those who have experienced failure can work towards recovery. In fact, many great historical figures achieved success after the age of forty. Young adults under the age of twenty-five who are able to identify their goals and work towards them can have a tremendous impact on the world and be remembered for their achievements.

As you can see, the issue of time is actually secondary. The primary concern is awareness, which can consume a significant amount of time. Once you reach a high level of self-awareness, including your personality, abilities, talents, and innermost desires, executing a plan for success will no longer be an issue. I have provided you with the key to success! The recipe for awareness that I have shared with you can significantly shorten your journey. Instead of taking years to gradually understand yourself, use goal engineering to unlock the secret. We all want to live a fulfilling life, but true age is determined by the knowledge we acquire, as it shortens our time of discovery. It's truly amazing when someone can give you valuable advice in an affordable book, which adds virtual years to your life.

What is True Success?

Success, as defined by goal engineering, involves finding balance among the five components we mentioned earlier. This means that these factors (money, health, emotions, knowledge, and relationships) eventually become equally important.

A truly successful person is someone who is wealthy, healthy, happy with positive emotions, knowledgeable, and holds a prestigious social status all at the same time. This is what it means to be truly successful, whereas someone who only possesses one or some of these components is still on the path towards success.

However, there is a problem with this definition as it suggests that people cannot achieve all five of these things. This may seem to contradict the idea of the goal code, which states that people differ in the personality traits that lead to success. Although it may seem contradictory, to understand how all 120 personality types can balance their five components, you need to focus on the following dialogue between logic and curiosity.

Curiosity: Can health bring in money?

Logic: Yes, here's the proof:

- A healthy person is capable of working using their body.
- Working using the body is a way to earn money.
- Therefore, a healthy person is capable of earning money.

Curiosity: But money cannot buy health.

Logic: Why not?

Curiosity: Because health is sacred and gifted, it cannot be acquired with money.

Logic: That was true in ancient times, but today you can buy health. The rich can afford treatment in the most expensive hospitals in the world, they can even have organ transplants, regain their vision and be cured of most diseases. The situation is improving day by day thanks to scientific advancements. Additionally, the wealthy follow an advanced dietary system due to their purchasing power. They have time for exercise because they don't work all the time, and they are less psychologically stressed, which enables them to prevent some stress-related illnesses. Therefore, money can buy health or at least improve it.

Curiosity: Money can't buy happiness.

Logic: Do you think the poor are happier than the rich?

Curiosity: There are poor people who are happy.

Logic: Is it genuine happiness or just a way to numb the pain? Do they wish to become rich to truly enjoy life and experience real happiness?

Curiosity: Yes, they do wish to become rich, but there are poor people who live contentedly.

Logic: If they live contentedly, that means they are rich. Lack of money leads to a feeling that can only be numbed with mental anesthesia and pretending that nothing has happened.

Curiosity: But there are unhappy rich people.

Logic: Yes, that's true.

Curiosity: Why aren't they happy? This means that money doesn't buy happiness.

Logic: Because they haven't bought happiness yet. Those who have money are supposed to be able to engage in activities that bring positive feelings, including happiness.

Curiosity: Okay, happiness doesn't buy money.

Logic: Can you change the word "buy"? Because money is what "buys" things.

Curiosity: Okay, happiness doesn't bring or generate money.

Logic: That's not true! All positive emotions, including psychological happiness, have an impact on one's mindset. They make a person more efficient, instill confidence in investment decisions, foster optimism and ambition, and ultimately contribute to financial success. While the connection may not be immediately apparent, a closer focus reveals the influence of positive emotions on wealth accumulation.

Curiosity: Okay, what about knowledge and relationships?

Logic: Do you want to take two subjects at once to speed things up? That's not a problem because I can answer that. Knowledge enables the creation of a professional product, whether it's an invention, a book, or anything else. Specialized knowledge (marketing), which is a type of knowledge, enables the sale of a product. Selling a product brings in money. Therefore, knowledge is capable of bringing in money. And the reverse is also true, as the person with money can purchase training courses that are not available to the general public, thus buying valuable knowledge that is not available to everyone. As for relationships, it's no secret that everyone loves and respects the person with money, or at least they can protect themselves and buy followers and...

Curiosity: But there are wealthy people who are hated.

Logic: This does not mean that they have not been able to build relationships with others. Even Jesus and Muhammad (peace be upon them), who I believe are among the most famous and followed figures, have haters and enemies. There are no absolute relationships, just as there is no person who owns all the money in the world or all knowledge! You must specify the quantity or put it in the required context and not leave it like this.

Curiosity: Okay, continue.

Logic: Complex and wide relations enable a person to gain clients and thus make money. Do you want to continue with the other pairs: (health-knowledge), (health-emotions), etc.?

Curiosity: No, I understand the method you're using now.

Succeeding in one particular field can often pave the way for success in other areas. Someone who excels at controlling their emotions will handle situations professionally, have a body that can resist stress-induced illnesses, and quickly gain customers, followers, and friends. Additionally, having a positive attitude towards money can increase one's chances of accumulating wealth. Similarly, all five components of success can lead to achievement in other areas.

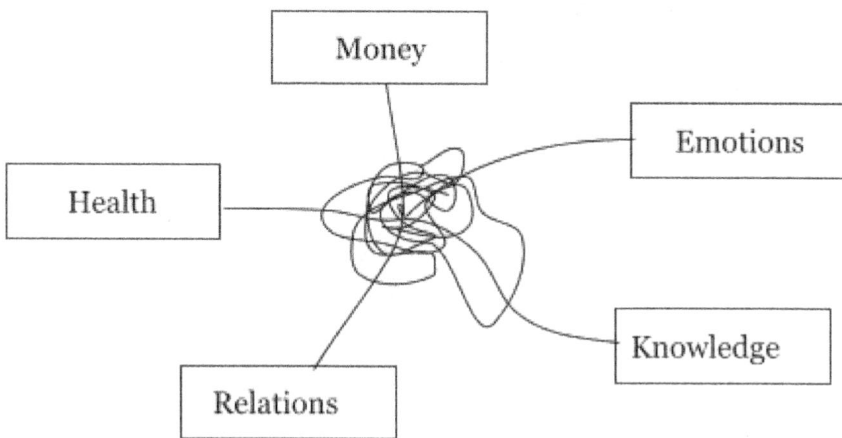

Therefore, it is unwise to focus on your weaknesses. Instead, focus on using your strengths as the foundation to build upon and acquire the other components of success later. Even if you desire all components now, it is important to prioritize and pursue them in a strategic order. If you fixate on money, which may not be the driving force behind your actions, you will likely fail. You may not possess the same qualifications and ability to work long hours and take risks like successful entrepreneurs do. By focusing on your main strengths and goals, you can accelerate success in a specific area and then apply it to other fields.

Consider entrepreneurs who not only excel at building projects but also dedicate their time to charitable endeavors due to their passion for making a positive impact. On the other hand, imagine influencers who prioritize their status and relationships with others over monetary gain, yet still possess greater wealth compared to entrepreneurs. These individuals may take on roles that do not align with their strengths and desires, leading to failure or delayed success. It is important to fully understand your capabilities and desires to achieve success in a way that is authentic and fulfilling to you.

What about the “Secret”?

"The Secret," written by Rhonda Byrne, is one of my favorite books. However, can we utilize the law of attraction to determine if we are on the right path? Our book isn't about passing judgment on the effectiveness of the law; rather, it focuses on our personal experiences that either validate or challenge its validity. Within this law, there is a certain logic to explain success and failure :

- Think about what you want and make it clear.
- Ask for what you desire.
- Feel good about your desires.
- Believe that you have already received what you want.
- Act as if you have already obtained it.
- The universe will align events, people, and circumstances to help you achieve your desires.

The purpose of this law is to make goal achievement an automatic and unconscious process. When you have strong belief in your ability to achieve something, you may not consciously notice the efforts you are making towards that goal. If your aim is to become wealthy, follow these steps:

- Think and believe that you already have enough.
- Develop the same habits and mindset as successful individuals.
- Notice and seize opportunities that can lead to wealth.
- Unconsciously let go of the possibility of failure, which will propel you towards success.

While this strategy is indeed powerful, I believe it primarily emphasizes the spiritual aspect of goal achievement. Maintaining such a mindset without engaging in tangible activities is useless. One issue with some proponents of the law of attraction is that they often teach that "anything" is possible and attainable, disregarding the realistic aspects of a goal.

Consider this: Can you imagine yourself flying, truly believe that you are flying, and then manifest the ability to fly? While it is true that human beings invented airplanes to fulfill the desire to fly, the dream itself evolved and adapted over time. Initially, humans aimed to fly like birds, but the pragmatic world ultimately pursued a more feasible goal: building a machine capable of flight. The law of attraction cannot override the physical laws that govern our reality.

Besides, you can not attract things that are far from you in a short period of time, because your mind will reject it. Can you imagine yourself a doctor and be so in a short period of time if you don't follow the steps that any doctor followed? So what causes the dream to be a reality? Is it "wanting to become a doctor" or "doing what is needed? ". If you are a math teacher at school and want to be a doctor, can you just believe that you are able to do so?

Another problem with this law is that it doesn't guide you in choosing the right goal. You can simply pick any objective, believe you deserve it, and voila, it supposedly manifests. However, this approach overlooks the crucial aspect of discerning a meaningful goal that aligns with your capabilities, passions, and purpose. After all, it's challenging to sustain continuous focus on something without an innate desire to achieve it. It is important to recognize that without an inherent drive, it becomes difficult to maintain the necessary determination and focus until the goal is manifested.

Having expressed my critique of this powerful law, I will now draw a comparison with goal engineering and subsequently provide guidance on how to achieve your goals.

Pros of The Law of Attraction

- Due to his spiritual beauty, people are naturally attracted to it with great speed.
- Provides hope and encouragement for people to continue on their journey.
- Assists in maintaining a positive mindset.
- Facilitates the achievement of goals through an unconscious process.

Pros of Goals Engineering

- Searching for effective strategies to achieve goals.
- Explaining the theory of goal achievement pragmatically
- Assisting individuals in maintaining a realistic and comprehensive perspective
- Identifying and showcasing individuals' skills, innate desires, strengths, and weaknesses
- Aiding in the selection of appropriate and attainable goals
- Convincing individuals of the futility of pursuing misguided goals.

Cons of The Law of Attraction

- Overly reliant on spirituality.
- Users may experience uncertainty regarding the effectiveness of the method.
- Lack of reliability in producing consistent results.
- Doubt may arise after experiencing multiple failures.
- Not compatible with the rational nature of humans, as it conflicts with the ongoing debate between the rational and irrational aspects of the mind.
- Does not take into consideration the specification of the user, skills and intellectual level.

Cons of Goals Engineering

- Excessively logical, rational, and focused on the material aspect, disregarding the spiritual dimension of human nature, where equations like" if a+b=a+c, then a=c" are solely based on abstract robotic considerations.
- Harsh on people who want an easy life, as it tries to open eyes to reality.
- Confining individuals to their existing skills and predetermined roles, suggesting that success is solely achieved by leveraging what one already possesses.

Please note that while the goals engineering approach may appear to stifle individuals' desires and confine them to their existing skills and innate roles under the notion that "success equals utilizing what you have," it paradoxically serves as an encouragement for individuals to push their limits and strive for greatness within their chosen path.

What is The Solution Then ?

Goals engineering strongly advises adopting a pragmatic and realistic approach, akin to various engineering disciplines. However, it also recognizes the value of incorporating spirituality. I highly recommend utilizing the law of attraction as a tool to support you on your journey.

Personally, I employ it to manifest my desires, but I acknowledge that a solid plan, dedication, and discipline are crucial for achieving what you want. The law of attraction reinforces the notion that your diligent efforts are guided and purposeful. When you soar, remember to employ both wings: the practical and the spiritual aspects.

Be mindful when selecting goals that align with your capabilities and are grounded in realism. You have the freedom to dream big, such as aspiring to compete with Elon Musk in establishing Mars colonies. However, it's important to recognize that achieving such a goal would require being in close proximity to him and having the necessary resources and expertise.

CHAPTER 7

Goals Filtering

Humans always yearn for more in every aspect of life. We possess a rich imagination of the ideal beings we aspire to be. However, a challenge arises when we attempt to outsmart nature in certain ways. Over thousands of years, humans have constructed a complex and luxurious world, unbeknownst to nature, which has followed the laws of survival in a defensive manner for millions of years.

The evolution of humanity and the development of this intricate civilization stem from our pursuit of perfection and the desire to rectify what we perceive as nature's shortcomings. Interestingly, nature's superior intelligence lies in its relentless endeavor to enhance human existence. It sets traps and reveals deficiencies in all aspects, urging us to utilize our intellect to improve the circumstances. Through this process, nature benefits and evolves in ways unbeknownst to it, while humans gradually move closer to a more perfect life.

The inherent intelligence of human beings, coupled with their fertile imagination and relentless pursuit of perfection, can sometimes lead individuals to withdraw from taking action and instead dwell within their inner world.

They may immerse themselves in dreams and aspirations that seem elusive within the confines of natural laws. Yet, over time, these dreams and aspirations can be realized, as evidenced by humanity's centuries-long yearning for flight, ultimately conquering nature's inclination to keep them grounded through the invention of iron machines that allow for air travel.

However, let me clarify that I am not referring to such grand collective dreams. I am speaking of individual dreams and aspirations—those personal desires that each person seeks to fulfill within the finite span of their life. It is important to recognize that a significant portion of our existence is consumed by childhood, sleep, and meeting basic needs.

So, the question arises: Can individuals, under such circumstances, achieve their individual dreams? Does it hinge on the nature of the dream itself or the necessary tools and resources? Let us be candid— collective dreams have indeed materialized throughout human history, but they often required tens of thousands of years to come to fruition, with each generation building upon the dreams of the preceding one. However, the realization of individual dreams within a prescribed timeframe poses a formidable challenge.

That's why it's important for humans to diminish the arrogance they mistake for intelligence, temper their fertile imagination, and control their dreams when approaching nature on an individual level. Many of the aspirations people have may not be attainable goals because, as I mentioned earlier, the human mind often fixates on perfection and overestimates its intelligence, overlooking the constraints imposed by nature.

Wishes Vs Goals

A wish is a comprehensive term for everything a person desires and dreams of achieving, even if it contradicts the laws of nature, such as wishing to return to youth after aging or desiring immortality. It cannot be definitively stated that these wishes cannot be realized in the long run, as humans often find solutions as they always do—who knows? However, what we agree on is that the available time frame for a generation or an individual is usually not sufficient to achieve such a wish.

So, there are different types of wishes:
Wishes that are achievable in the user's life/lives:

- Buying a dream house, for example.
- Winning a Nobel Prize.
- Discovering a new vaccine.
- Establishing a successful company.

Wishes that are not achievable within the available time frame but can be partially realized or have an equivalent achievement:

- Living on the moon. It may not be possible to achieve it quickly, but partial realization such as traveling to the moon or planting a plant there is possible.
- Creating a complete human. It may not be possible for scientists and doctors, but currently, organ transplantation or creating intelligent robots is achievable, or even human cloning.

Wishes that are entirely unachievable or it is uncertain whether humans can overcome their impossibility:

- Resurrecting the dead.
- Reversing aging.
- Making animals talk.

Let's set aside the third category as it falls outside the scope of goal engineering principles. The second category, on the other hand, is what propels humanity's advancement, although it tends to encompass collective aspirations rather than individual ones. While we may touch upon them to some extent, specialized goal engineering for this particular type of desires differs from our intended focus of study. The first category is of utmost importance in this book because it encompasses numerous individual goals that exemplify engineering principles more prominently.

So, what exactly are goals? They are attainable desires in the lives of users, as the means to achieve them are either known or can be studied. Additionally, users have access to the necessary tools such as time, natural laws, resources, and knowledge. Hence, goals can be regarded as a specific subset of wishes. To differentiate goals from wishes, it is essential to establish appropriate and clear criteria that we all agree upon.

Goals: Miniature Aspects of Wishes

When you ask someone about the amount of money they desire, they often imagine large sums without being able to specify an achievable amount based on the resources available now or in the future. Similarly, when you inquire about their health, they want to be free from all diseases, protected from any ailments, and maintain perpetual youth and well-being, painting an exaggerated and vague picture. As we mentioned earlier, this stems from the human desire for perfection, combined with an imagination and intelligence that surpasses the limitations of nature. Dreaming is a wonderful thing, but let's break down those long-term wishes into smaller, more realistic goals - these are the ones that truly matter.

Do you wish to attain an infinite amount of money? Or do you have a specific sum in mind, like a hundred thousand dollars, a million dollars, or something similar? As for your health, do you desire absolute well-being, or is it about maintaining your current health and gradually improving by addressing specific health issues you may face?

Do you notice how goals are like miniature parts of wishes? When goals accumulate, they bring us closer to fulfilling a wish. However, before we can achieve the wish itself, we must first attain those individual goals.

Goals are Logical, Wishes are Emotions

Wishes often stem from emotions, whereas the term "goals" specifically refers to those wishes that have been filtered from excessive emotions and can be deemed logical. In other words, goals are logical wishes that can be articulated and their achievement can be explained in a logical manner.

The most important aspect of logical progression is that it is explainable. You cannot explain to people how to find the perfect life partner who has no flaws, because that is a clear wish.

However, you can demonstrate to people that there is no perfect person, but you can find someone with specific qualities by giving examples of individuals you have met or know, and how you are getting closer each time to the partner you want to be with.

You cannot explain how to obtain a million dollars within an hour when you have no business or money in your bank account, but you can explain step by step how to achieve it if you have ample time over months or even years, or if you are already a multimillionaire.

Goals Come with Flaws

The distinguishing factor between a goal and a wish is that a goal inherently carries imperfections or flaws, and it's important to accept them as part of the process. If your desire is to attain a significant amount of money without encountering any challenges, difficulties, then it is more akin to a wish rather than a goal. Flaws are essential components of a goal, and it is through acknowledging them that we can truly classify it as such. If you perceive a particular goal as flawless, devoid of any negatives or shortcomings, it still falls into the category of wishes, and it becomes necessary for you to recognize and acknowledge any concealed flaws.

SMART Goals

There is a well-known principle called the SMART goals principle that can be applied to distinguish between a goal and a wish.

1. Goals should be Specific, meaning they are clearly defined. You should be able to describe the goal in a single, clear sentence that is understood by everyone and is specific and not general.

2. Goals should be Measurable, meaning there are indicators that show progress towards the goal.

3. Goals should be Attainable using the resources at hand. This means that the components required to create the product associated with the goal must either already be manufactured or can be demonstrated as feasible through the scientific advancements made by the relevant parties.

4. Goals should be Relevant, which means that the person pursuing the goal must have expertise in the field to maintain the project or have a relevant background.

5. The goal should be Time-bound, indicating that the timeframe for its achievement is defined, and it should be within the lifespan of the individual pursuing the goal.

For example:

"I want to become rich."

This is a wish because it is general and not specific.

"I want to accumulate a sufficient amount of money."

It is starting to become clear to the listener that the intended richness is about acquiring a sufficient cash amount. However, this cannot be classified as a goal as it requires additional conditions in addition to the requirement of specificity. This wish still needs to be broken down or fragmented to become clearer.

"I want to earn $100,000".

The wish is now clear and measurable, it is more quantified but still not considered as a correct goal since we do not know if it is doable.

"I want to accumulate $100,000 without doing anything."

The goal is unachievable because there is no clear means to accomplish it.

"I want to accumulate $100,000 by creating a new chemical substance."

The goal is still unachievable because the available knowledge does not allow for it.

"I want to raise $100,000 by establishing a foreign language school."

Establishing projects has proven to be successful, and many have earned substantial amounts of money from such ventures. The goal is clear, measurable, and achievable, but we do not know if the goal seeker is capable of accomplishing it.

"I want to raise $100,000 by establishing a foreign language school, but I have no knowledge about languages or establishing schools. I am a cook."

This goal is achievable, but it is not the same goal that was initially outlined. It requires the same previous process of deconstruction and refinement because it is closer to a wish rather than a goal.

If the project owner aims to generate income through a language school but lacks knowledge in this field, they would need to invest substantial amounts of money. In this case, it cannot be considered as establishing a project but rather as investing in one. This contradicts the specific goal mentioned earlier, which implies a desire to generate income from scratch or with minimal expenses. Hence, we can conclude that this is a different goal, not the specific goal mentioned earlier.

"I want to raise $100,000 by establishing a foreign language school online. I am a Spanish teacher and I have friends who are language teachers."

The goal is now relevant to the subject, but we do not know when it will be achieved or its time relevance, and progress cannot be measured over time. Therefore, we cannot call it a goal.

This is indeed a goal, but it could easily transform into a mere wish if there is no proper time plan in place for its accomplishment. While the goal aligns with the subject matter, the uncertainty regarding its time frame, its temporal relationship, and the ability to track progress over time make it challenging to categorize it as a definitive goal.

"I aim to raise $100,000 by establishing a foreign language school. It may take approximately two years to achieve this goal."

Additionally, the project owner provides an explanation:

"The initial six months will be devoted to content creation, followed by another six months for the website, the app and material development. The subsequent six months will center around marketing, establishing a sales network, and acquiring clients. The final six months will be dedicated to error correction and scaling the business.."

The goal now is :

- Clear
- Measurable
- Attainable
- Relevant
- Time-bound

Now it becomes clear to you that a goal is distinguished from a mere wish. You can practice this. In the first chapter, you have written most of the goals you want to achieve.

Now, evaluate them using these criteria and ask yourself if what you desire is realistic and logical goals or just wishes and emotions.

Please be aware that there is no need to provide an extensive description of the goal. However, it is crucial to ensure a clear understanding that all these aspects have been fulfilled.

Simplified Goals Filtering

While the SMART principle is useful for evaluating and assessing goals, it has limitations and may restrict individual desires. Although the principle is logical, it lacks flexibility and fails to consider the individual's unique personality and circumstances.

While it can be applied to define goals for companies or groups, a clearer and simpler standard is needed when dealing with the intricate realm of human emotions. The SMART principle does not guarantee the achievability of individual goals as it overlooks the human element, including personal characteristics and abilities.

We previously mentioned the method you should use to evaluate goals, which is: Do your wishes align with your goal scale? In a language learning application project, the SMART principle focuses on project effectiveness but does not emphasize the individual's talents and ability to overcome obstacles.

We can assess the achievability of the goal by asking different questions than those posed by the principle, such as:

1. What is the type of the goal?
2. Where does the driving force responsible for achieving this goal reside?
3. Does the goal owner have significant opportunities to achieve it based on his innate skills?

The goal is primarily financial in nature. If the goal owner is an entrepreneur, regardless of their interest in languages, there is a high probability of achieving it. Entrepreneurs are driven by their focus on monetary gains and their ambitious nature. The primary engine helps them stay on track towards achieving the goal. Among entrepreneurs, founders—who possess the knowledge engine at the second rank—are the most capable of achieving the goal, as they learn quickly while pursuing it. However, this doesn't imply that individuals in other roles cannot achieve the goal.

Marketers excel at promoting the product, but their work begins after the project is completed. On the other hand, managers excel at project management and ensuring successful completion. Although they are not directly involved in development, they are responsible for issuing orders and coordinating various components. Their physical energy for work tends to be lower due to the importance of maintaining a stable rhythm, which is influenced by the 2nd engine "health."

Investors have a lower chance of achieving such a project, as they prefer to minimize physical fatigue. This is due to the fact that the health engine must be lower on the scale, considering that the first and second ranks are already occupied. Their primary focus is on anticipating success, investing capital in the project, and maintaining emotional control. Inventors belonging to the scholar sect community also possess the potential to accomplish such a project. They emphasize quality more than profitability, with their goal being "How can it be achieved?" rather than "How can it be profitable ?" Founders are likely to alter the project if they see greater profit opportunities, whereas inventors concentrate on enhancing the product and making it the best it can be, regardless of expected profits.

Perhaps you've noticed how certain goal scales provide their owners with greater opportunities to achieve specific goals, regardless of their clarity. What may be a goal for one faction or group is merely a wish for others. Imagine if someone from the spiritualists, like a devoted ascetic, were to consider or be told that this is a good project. Do you think they would complete the project until the end? And even if they did, do you believe it would be of the same quality as what members of the inventor community produce, or generate profits comparable to what founders have achieved?

Understanding and comprehending the goal scale not only enables us to understand ourselves, but it can also be used as a criterion to differentiate between a mere wish and a true goal. We are on a journey in search of meaning in life and the pursuit of a goal that we are content with before surrendering to mortality when it arrives because we have fulfilled what we truly needed to accomplish in this life. This journey requires effective tools, and goal engineering will allow you to do just that, as I am speaking from extensive experience and years of contemplating on this subject.

But what if someone has a different purpose for this project other than money:

What is the type of goal?

Emotions, I want to feel that I have accomplished something, and that is a wonderful feeling.

Where does the engine responsible for achieving this goal lie?

In the first position, the emotional engine is in the first position for me.

Does the goal owner have a great chance of achieving it?

I am resilient and capable of achieving this goal because what drives me is not money, but emotions.

In this scenario, the individual from the spiritualist sect harnesses their unique abilities and skills to pursue a goal with a different nature. If their intention behind choosing this goal is genuinely sincere, they will find joy in the journey. It may take them longer to accomplish this goal compared to entrepreneurs, as they do not possess the same level of energy and stamina to withstand fatigue.

However, gradually, they will lay the foundations of this project and derive satisfaction from the emotions that arise as the project evolves. In essence, their desired outcome is not a language learning plateforme, but rather the sense of achievement that comes with each milestone. Although it is uncommon for spiritual individuals to embark on such projects and think about them, they can still successfully complete the project by avoiding an internal focus on money and profit. Once the project is completed, they can enlist the support of marketers to generate profits from the product. By doing so, they achieve two goals simultaneously: experiencing positive emotions and earning money.

If they blindly or stubbornly choose to rush through the project and compete with entrepreneurs, they will inevitably fail because they won't be able to withstand the negative emotions that overpower them. Their desire is to always maintain a positive state and embrace life as it is, without obstinacy. However, their inclination to nurture positive emotions will hinder their progress because they are simply not aligned with that particular goal. They have prioritized their weaker driving force, "Money," while neglecting the stronger one. Consequently, they won't succeed in such a project. They are not meant to be solely focused on accumulating wealth and completing projects; rather, they aim to relish each moment and embrace all positive emotions, avoiding anything that disrupts the tranquility of their lives.

This does not imply that they will live in poverty. As mentioned before, they will cleverly find a way to enjoy life and disregard the matter of money, allowing their emotions to create a product that can be sold or generate income without conflicting with their inner feelings.

This principle applies to all goals and sects. Each individual must enhance their judgment and carefully select the goals they wish to achieve, understanding that there are also responsibilities they must fulfill because that is their role in life. To attain what they desire, they must offer what they are meant to give and fulfill their purpose as nature has predicted. This doesn't mean they do not have complete control over anything, but there is a price they must pay to obtain what they want.

If your calling is to be a scholar but you aspire to be wealthy, you won't achieve wealth unless you acquire extensive knowledge. However, this isn't a requirement for entrepreneurs. There are uneducated individuals who have become rich due to their unwavering entrepreneurial mindset, not because they possess superior understanding compared to others. Similarly, if you're a successful entrepreneur, you won't be able to compete with scientists in their specialized fields. If you desire to do so, you'll need to invest a significant amount of money, effort, and time in specialized learning centers, while scientists effortlessly delve into numerous learning resources and are self-taught learners.. Moreover, their understanding reaches a level where they can rectify presented information and establish theories that challenge commonly held beliefs, or even write books that you will purchase.

Emphasizing your strengths is crucial in goal setting because achieving success in one of the five pillars facilitates obtaining the others effortlessly. You won't succeed by merely imitating exceptional individuals, but rather by cultivating your own exceptional qualities. Then, you can strive for balance in your life. In this manner, nature will provide you with what you desire because you have fulfilled your obligations and played your role. If you refuse, the only person to blame is yourself.

Take the necessary time to meticulously evaluate every goal before embarking on its execution. Throughout this process, it is crucial that you refrain from succumbing to negativity. Starting with pessimism or a sense of disappointment will inevitably impede your progress, even if the goal lies well within your capabilities. While it is important to maintain a logical mindset, do not permit your preprogrammed thoughts to dictate a role for you in life that contradicts your true purpose. By leveraging your strengths and making astute goal choices, the achievement of your aspirations becomes an irrefutable certainty. Armed with the ability to devise your own strategies, you will persevere unwaveringly along your chosen path, fully cognizant of your desires and with unwavering confidence in your capacity to bring them to fruition. Obstacles will be surmounted, solutions to problems will be found, and your innate strengths will empower you to skillfully navigate the twists and turns, ultimately culminating in the realization of the meticulously designed goal you have set before yourself.

If you fail, it means that the goal was just a wish or that you approached it without any strategy, relying only on your weaknesses. Keep in mind that what may be a wish for you is a goal for others, like your desire to win a Nobel Prize. However, individuals within the scientific community consider it an actual goal, and they have the ability to achieve it. No matter how small the wish, it becomes challenging to attain if it doesn't align with your capabilities. Therefore, you need to find alternative goals that you can accomplish. By pursuing those goals, you will gradually move closer to realizing your original wish.

This chapter has provided you with valuable insights into the concept of goal evaluation, which involves examining your goals and assessing their alignment with your own aspirations. It's important to start immediately by evaluating your goals, analyzing your past experiences, and understanding the reasons behind your past failures. Once you become adept at selecting smaller goals and aligning your perspective with your ultimate life goal, you can embark on discovering your role in this journey called life.

CHAPTER 8

Modeling & Validation

Categorizing goals based on their sources, prioritizing them, filtering through them, understanding individual differences, and analyzing the underlying links are all essential processes for choosing the right goals that one will not later regret pursuing. But how can an individual ensure their success? How can they predict the outcome of their goal setting ?

Are there methods to guarantee that all their efforts, ambitions, plans, and dreams do not go to waste? Engaging in a thorough simulation to anticipate the future and evaluate their success rate and competitive opportunities is necessary. There is no harm in experimenting and learning from experiences, but the real danger lies in selecting goals that are ultimately destructive

Goals that are incompatible with an individual's abilities can be detrimental. These goals can be classified into the following categories:

1. Goals that fail to meet essential criteria, such as clarity, feasibility, and time management.
2. Goals that individuals desire but their inherent weaknesses prevent them from pursuing them effectively. These are the most hazardous types of destructive goals.
3. Goals that individuals are capable of achieving, but they lack personal motivation or enthusiasm for them.
4. Imitative goals that are not aligned with the individual's genuine personality
5. Goals that do not align with the environment in which the individual resides.

Many times, people struggle to select the right goal because they prioritize their desires and neglect their abilities and weaknesses. There are techniques individuals can use to reinforce their assessments of their aptitude for achieving a goal and its alignment with their own characteristics.

The Proof to Back Down

The purpose of the backward reasoning is to infer that you are capable of achieving a goal if it aligns with you and you belong to the most fortunate faction to achieve it. The method gradually tries to prove that you are capable of achieving the goal through the following steps:

1. Choosing a specific goal.
2. Applying the filtering principle as we discussed in the previous chapter.
3. Searching for factors that facilitate the achievement of the goal.
4. Selecting the faction that aligns most with this goal and has a natural ease in achieving it.
5. Assessing your distance or affiliation to this faction.

There needs to be a harmony between a goal that meets specific criteria and the qualifications of the person striving to achieve it. This harmony holds the key to successful goal attainment and the ability to persist in the face of challenges over the long haul.

In this context, it implies that an individual's knowledge and inherent skills align with the demands of the goal. Furthermore, their desire for this particular type of goal is strong enough to keep them focused, patient when confronted with obstacles, and even find enjoyment in the process for an extended period of time. It's also important to note that their weaknesses should not be essential as strengths required by the goal. You might have noticed that we are gradually returning to the concept of the five engines.

The individual's skills and latent abilities are highly prominent in the first and second engines, their desire and comfort are centered in the third engine, while their weaknesses and unawareness come into play in the fourth and fifth engines. This suggests that eligibility, in this context, involves aligning your goal hierarchy with the requirements of the goal.

Let's provide some examples of compatibility between goals and different types of individuals.

Authoring a book on healthy nutrition and selling it requires more than mere monetary considerations. Rather than spending months or years writing, obtaining copyright, and then selling the book, a more straightforward approach is to directly sell ready-made books for financial gain. However, a true author should be driven by a passion for writing and possess the ability to navigate the anxieties that come with completing a book. Furthermore, a solid grasp of medical, biological, and nutritional concepts is essential, enabling the author to conduct thorough research from reliable sources and effectively communicate and simplify complex ideas for readers. While writing proficiency is crucial, delegating the task of revising and editing to others is a viable option. The author's primary objective should be to enlighten and educate readers about health and proper nutrition, rather than solely focusing on selling the book, seeking fame, or accumulating wealth.

This signifies the following:

1. The author prioritizes health over financial gains.
2. The author's extensive knowledge motivates them to continuously learn and provide valuable insights, surpassing mere monetary pursuits.
3. Health takes precedence over building relationships or seeking direct fame.
4. The author possesses the emotional resilience to sustain their dedication over a prolonged period, transforming mundane writing into captivating entertainment.

Above all, Members of the doctors faction stand the best chance of accomplishing this goal. Their inherent concern for personal and public health, combined with a commitment to accurate information and the necessary patience, sets them apart.

1. Health		1. Health
2. Knowledge		2. Knowledge
3. Emotions	**OR**	3. Emotions
4. Relations		4. Money
5. Money		5. Relations

When it comes to certain factions and groups, this goal holds no significance, and they might not find any motivation to consider it as an objective. A destructive goal is one that seems attainable and lucrative but lacks one crucial element: an intense desire to achieve it or an understanding that their weaknesses align with the goal's requirements.

For some entrepreneurs, pursuing this goal would prove detrimental as they prioritize matters other than health and lack the patience required for such projects. They are driven by the pursuit of substantial material ventures that resonate with engine order:

1. Money
2. Knowledge
3. Relations
4. Sensations
5. Safety

An entrepreneur with this mindset might excel in creating a social media platform, but attempting to write a book on health would inevitably result in failure or even prove destructive for him.

Let's consider another example of a goal:

"I have a vision to establish a new religious movement and become a spiritual leader like Gandhi and others. My aim is to enlighten people about the profound happiness found within, surpassing the fleeting pleasures of the material world."

This goal would not resonate with individuals belonging to the entrepreneurial, sages, or scholars sects as it fundamentally contradicts their inclinations. While building a sizable community or religious sect may bring long-term gains, it would fail to capture the attention of entrepreneurs who prioritize direct, tangible outcomes or the pursuit of clearly defined objectives.

The sages and doctors, in particular, would not be drawn to such goals due to the inherent risks they pose. The patience required to establish a community of this nature entails physical exertion and exposes one's life to potential threats like physical attacks, imprisonment, or even assassination by opponents and enemies.

Those most inclined to undertake such a mission are predominantly affiliated with spiritualists, monks, or influencers. Influencers are driven by aspirations for fame, status, and admiration, while monks are motivated by a quest for spiritual fulfillment and a genuine desire to benefit others. They are deeply committed to assisting people in understanding their emotions and navigating life's challenges by focusing on the spirit rather than material possessions.

Let's explore a scenario where an entrepreneur, a sage, or scholar decides to pursue this goal, with their "emotions" and "relationships" engines ranked second in importance. In this case, they might demonstrate a certain level of resilience in their pursuit. However, their level of satisfaction may fall short compared to that of the spiritualist and influencer factions.

Now, if we consider a scenario where these engines rank fourth or fifth in importance, there would be minimal interest from users towards this particular goal. However, if these drives were to rank third in importance, the situation becomes more precarious. The individual would experience a strong desire to achieve the goal, but it may not align with their abilities or suit their weaknesses. Under such circumstances, the goal becomes not only destructive but also a futile endeavor, even if it manages to achieve partial success.

Let's consider another example: the dream of learning singing and music and attaining fame through it. This goal may ignite the desire of all factions:

- Entrepreneurs see it as an excellent opportunity to generate wealth.
- Wise individuals appreciate this profession due to its low physical energy requirements and minimal risks.
- Spiritualists derive enjoyment from the emotions and sensations that arise, fueling their dedication to learning and performing singing.
- Scholars are intrigued by the melody, the ability to compose, and the underlying complexity.
- Influencers are motivated by the allure of fame and status.

Although this goal is suitable for all factions, certain combinations must be more fortunate and aligned, particularly for creative individuals and celebrities within the spiritualist faction. They possess the greatest passion and sensitivity, which can act as a distraction from considering the obstacles that artists encounter on their journey.

The Reversed Engineering

Reverse engineering means dismantling a system and understanding its functioning and how it was assembled in order to use that knowledge in creating similar applications. There are multiple aspects of reverse engineering for goals that can be applied to live a better life, avoid destructive goals, and choose the best and most suitable goals that align with an individual's personality.

Analyzing the lives of successful individuals aids in comprehending the factors contributing to their goal accomplishments. It's important to note that not everyone you admire or respect will serve as a suitable role model. Some individuals may simply complement your strengths and weaknesses. Therefore, it is advisable to seek out someone whose personality aligns with yours to some degree or belongs to a similar category.

When searching for a suitable role model, consider finding a person who:

- They have achieved significant success.
- You genuinely like and admire them.
- You aspire to become like them.
- You are familiar with their biography.
- You feel a sense of similarity with them

Once you've chosen a personality that resonates with you, begin by analyzing and reverse-engineering it. Ask questions that help you understand the five engines within this individual:

- What kinds of goals pique the interest of this personality?
- What drives them to achieve all these accomplishments?
- How can you verify and validate their motivations through their statements?
- What challenges and obstacles did they face, and how did they overcome them?
- What sets me apart from this personality? Can it be emulated?

Maintain a neutral stance and avoid answering the questions based on enthusiasm, a craving for success, or mere imitation. Your goal is to diagnose the system and comprehend it in order to create something similar. If you realize that this person is fundamentally different from you, seek out a more suitable personality.

It's misguided to mimic someone who possesses different skills and talents than you, but you can certainly gain insights from their experiences. When you discover a personality that aligns perfectly with your own, you may feel a sense of bewilderment and wonder why you haven't been able to accomplish similar things despite having the capability. Finding your life's purpose or a captivating goal will make your heart beat fervently, as if something is telling you, "You should strive to be like this”.

Does the personality that resembles yours resemble someone like Elon Musk, for example? From a young age, he had an interest in both money and creating things. He began by developing simple systems before progressing to create more complex ventures such as PayPal, and later on, he founded giant companies in the electric car (Tesla) and space travel (SpaceX) industries! There's no doubt that he firmly falls into one of these two factions.

The category of entrepreneurs, particularly founders:

1. Money
2. Knowledge
3. *******
4. *******
5. *******

Or scholars, particularly inventors:

1. Knowledge
2. Money
3. *******
4. *******
5. *******

To determine the order of the remaining engines, it would require closely following his life for an extended period or subjecting him to the same set of questions and tests presented in Chapter 2. We don't care much about that now because we'll focus on the goals he set.

His initial objective is to create and market his own inventions. He has set a distinct and measurable goal, with a defined timeframe for assessing his progress. Once he confirmed his capability to achieve small goals, he embarked on creating and selling larger products, always with calculated risks. These endeavors align with his desires, abilities, and interests, just as his previous successful goals did. He leverages various resources to expedite his progress.

Some of Elon musk declarations about money:

- "I actually don't care about money. I believe in the mission of Tesla, SpaceX, and SolarCity, and I'm trying to do what I can to have the biggest impact on society."
- "Money is a means to an end. I would like to have financial freedom, but it's not an end in itself. I want to make a difference."
- "I don't create companies for the sake of creating companies, but to get things done."
- "If something is important enough, even if the odds are against you, you should still do it."
- "The value of money is to fuel the cause, not to be the cause."
- "The first step is to establish that something is possible; then probability will occur."
- I'd like to think that I've got enough money to make sure my kids are taken care of, and that they'll never need to worry about money, but I'm not buying a mega-yacht."

- "Starting and growing a business is as much about innovation, drive, and determination as it is about the money."

Some of Elon musk declarations about knowledge:

- "I think it's very important to have a feedback loop, where you're constantly thinking about what you've done and how you could be doing it better."
- "Constantly seek criticism. A well-thought-out critique of whatever you're doing is as valuable as gold."
- "It's very important to like the people you work with, otherwise life [and learning] will be quite miserable."
- "I don't spend my time pontificating about high-concept things; I spend my time solving engineering and manufacturing problems."
- "If you're trying to create a company, it's like baking a cake. You have to have all the ingredients in the right proportion."
- "Failure is an option here. If things are not failing, you're not innovating enough."
- "It's OK to have your eggs in one basket as long as you control what happens to that basket."
- "I think most people can learn a lot more than they think they can. They sell themselves short without trying."
- I'm interested in things that change the world or that affect the future"

After examining his statements, it appears evident that Elon Musk prioritizes learning over the pursuit of money. Despite his substantial wealth, he regards money as merely a means to create valuable assets for the betterment of humanity. His primary objective is to be recognized and rewarded for his intellect and contributions in areas such as artificial intelligence, space exploration, technology, and solving significant global challenges.

Instead of utilizing money as an ultimate goal, he adopts a defensive approach towards it. Consequently, I would categorize Elon Musk as an inventor rather than a founder entrepreneur. His drive originates from comprehending the intricacies of how things operate before embarking on their execution. Elon Musk serves as an example, but you can choose any individual whose qualities resonate with you. Perhaps it's Angelina Jolie, Albert Einstein, Arnold Schwarzenegger, or even Jesus.

The initial step in this process involves ensuring that you share at least a common faction, making it more effective to have all five engines in the same sequence. Once you have thoroughly understood your model personality and reverse-engineered it, you can assess whether you are capable of undertaking similar endeavors. Rather than replicating his projects, you can start emulating his style.

If your intuition strongly suggests that pursuing something will not be worthwhile, trust that instinct and refrain from wasting your time on it. Your inner calling in this life is guiding you and telling you, "This is not what I truly desire.". Strike a balance between spirituality and reality, avoiding the extremes of being too closed off to the real world or becoming a mere robot.

CHAPTER 9

Energy Transfer

Similar to any engine, energy is transferred among the five motors in order to carry out a particular task. Understanding this principle is very important before designing the final plan to be executed.

When a member of any sect is in their normal state, they allocate more energy to the primary engine. This becomes crucial when pursuing goals within the same category. For instance, if a goal requires hard work, entrepreneurs naturally tend to persist because their energy is primarily focused on the first engine.

If the energy is distributed among the remaining engines, they will feel less motivated to pursue the same goal and may develop different inclinations towards other types of goals. It is important to maintain control over these dynamics, as when they wish to achieve goals in different categories such as happiness, for instance, they must effectively transfer the energy to the emotion engine.

Failing to achieve goals outside the primary engine's category is attributed to an ineffective energy transfer. While you cannot alter your affiliation with a sect or faction, you can enhance your skills to a level that allows you to make use of the lower engines on your scale effectively.

Transferring Energy to Money

If you aim to increase your earnings, you must concentrate all the distributed energy solely on the money engine. This entails ceasing the functioning of the other engines, allowing the money engine to operate at its maximum capacity.

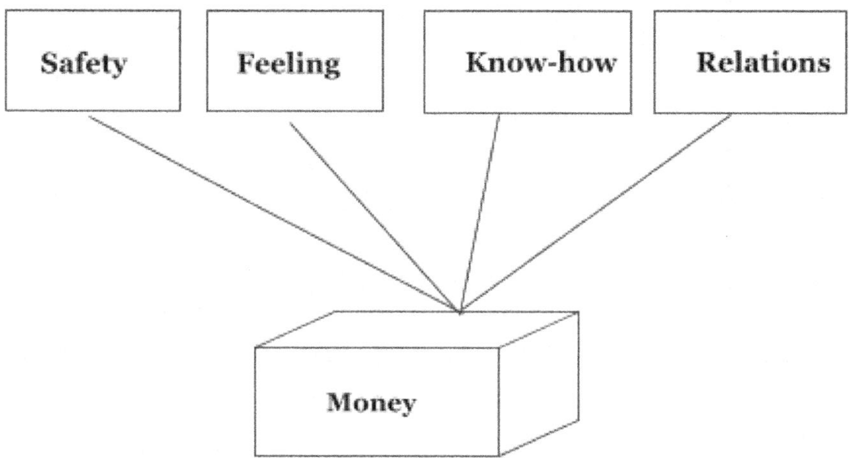

If you prioritize safety, maintain a sedentary lifestyle, consistently get enough sleep, and avoid fatigue, it may positively impact your overall health. However, it could potentially hinder your ability to earn money. When you channel your energy towards safety or health, it can become challenging to generate income. Making money often requires dedicated and strenuous efforts, involving long hours of hard work and active engagement. In essence, it comes down to a matter of energy transfer: either you focus on rest and prioritize safety, or you push yourself and focus on earning money.

The same applies to emotions. If you prioritize living in the moment, enjoying travel, and watching movies all the time, it may bring you happiness. However, it comes at the cost of neglecting other areas of life.

Active & Passive Energy Transfer

Transferring energy from health or emotion to money is considered a passive energy transfer since it involves sacrificing one motor to allow the other to function effectively. The same quantity of energy extracted from the safety or emotion engine is directly transferred to the money engine. For instance, if the health engine possesses 100 joules of energy, an equal or lesser amount is borrowed to empower the money engine in accomplishing its designated task.

The knowledge and relation engines operate on the same principle, allowing you to trade the time and effort spent on learning for automated work that generates income. Similarly, by distancing yourself from social interactions, you can allocate more energy and time towards money-related endeavors. However, these two types of motors also operate using another mode: active energy transfer.

Active energy transfer refers to the process of harnessing energy from external sources and utilizing the relevant engine to inject that energy into the system. In this case, the knowledge and relation motors function as amplifiers, enhancing the overall energy input.

For instance, leveraging your connections as a sales and distribution channel can be an effective means of generating income. In this case, you are not solely relying on your own time and effort, but rather, you are tunneling an external form of energy and converting it into a usable form for the engine in need of it. you enable a significant amount of energy to be transferred efficiently, instead of relying solely on the limited internal energy.

The same principle applies to the knowledge engine as well. Rather than sacrificing your time and energy to acquire new knowledge, you can utilize both your own expertise and the knowledge of others as input energy for the motor engine to be used. By doing so, you enable a significant amount of energy to be transferred, thereby increasing the likelihood of generating income.

This explains why individuals affiliated with the founder and marketer factions in the entrepreneurs sect are generally more likely to earn money compared to investors and managers. The former factions are more inclined to employ active energy transfer methods in their pursuit of greater earning.

By nature, you are inclined to predominantly rely on passive modes of energy transfer. However, if you manage to develop your active energy transfer capabilities, you will be pleasantly surprised by the accelerated momentum generated by the motors in attaining success. By incorporating this mechanism, You can accomplish two goals at once. Firstly, using the motor in its natural state without passive transfer, and secondly, allowing the necessary motor to receive the energy flow it requires.

Transferring Energy to Health

According to the principle of energy transfer theory, all you need to do is reverse the impact of the motors you possess, enabling a greater flow of energy towards the health engine. It's important to note that the energy derived from the second and third ranks is more plentiful compared to the remaining ranks.

As you can observe, money can be passively transferred to health. It requires reversing all the activities that the money engine compels you to engage in. Rather than opting for cheap products to save a few cents, prioritize purchasing high-quality food and beneficial supplements.

<table>
<tr><th>Rank</th><th>Normal Motion</th><th>Reversed Motion</th></tr>
<tr><td>1st</td><td>Work hard
Take risks</td><td rowspan="3">1. Take breaks or Rest periodically.
2. Ensure your safety.
3. Avoid stressing yourself out.
4. Consider purchasing supplements.
5. Invest in high-quality food.
6. Make an investment in your body.</td></tr>
<tr><td>2nd</td><td>Resist fatigue
Lower expenses</td></tr>
<tr><td>3rd</td><td>Save money</td></tr>
<tr><td>4th</td><td>Do not care too much about money</td><td rowspan="2">The money engine in this category is not efficient in passive energy transfer since it is inherently dissipative or a stopped motor.</td></tr>
<tr><td>5th</td><td>Ignore money</td></tr>
</table>

Money within the 4th and 5th ranks possesses a lower amount of available energy to be transferred to health. As previously mentioned, it serves as a tool. It is evident that individuals who rely on this motor within these ranks already encounter financial challenges, leading us to conclude that the safety or health engine may hold a higher priority on the scale in most cases. Consequently, there is no actual need for passive energy transfer from these tools.

Relations can also be passively transferred. Limiting your interactions with others will undoubtedly contribute to your overall health. It reduces your exposure to stress, potential unhealthy eating habits they may have, and helps protect you by minimizing the risk of contagious viruses, for example.

The remaining motors, namely emotions and knowledge, can naturally operate actively. Experiencing positive emotions and well-being will undoubtedly contribute to your overall health. Additionally, acquiring knowledge about the body and medicine will enhance your ability to maintain good health.

Transferring Energy to Knowledge

Consider purchasing books or learning materials without overly concerning yourself with the price, as the most valuable knowledge often comes with a cost. Teachers and content creators invest significant time in enhancing the quality of their learning materials, alongside their own extensive learning journeys. Therefore, if you aspire to expand your knowledge, it is crucial to reverse the influence of the money engine. If it urges you to seek free resources, opt for the opposite approach and invest in a paid course. By transferring money to knowledge without hesitation, you are more likely to sustain your learning journey and acquire valuable information.

The same principle applies to emotions and body comfort, as learning can sometimes evoke negative feelings when acquiring necessary knowledge. It is important to allow yourself to experience discomfort at times in exchange for valuable information.

Learning often thrives in solitude and requires focused attention. This explains why introverts tend to exhibit higher levels of intelligence compared to extroverts. However, it's important to note that energy can also be actively transferred. Utilize your relationships to expand your knowledge, being selective in your interactions but remaining open to learning from every individual. Even our adversaries can offer valuable lessons and insights.

Transferring Energy to Emotions

You simply need to reverse the remaining engines to feel better. Saving money, working hard, investing, and being mindful of financial planning will contribute to achieving the goals related to the money category. On the other hand, Living in the moment, indulging in shopping, traveling, and spending money on things you desire can bring you joy.

Following a balanced diet, engaging in regular and disciplined sports training, prioritizing body care, and ensuring adequate sleep will contribute to achieving your health-related goals. Indulging in delicious meals, participating in risky games, and enjoying nightlife at parties and other unhealthy activities can provide an immediate sense of pleasure and satisfaction.

Acquiring the necessary knowledge for a job or specific tasks can sometimes feel tedious, but it significantly enhances an individual's overall knowledge. Following your passion and exploring your interests, being spontaneous, can contribute to a greater sense of well-being. It has been also suggested that individuals with lower intelligence tend to experience higher levels of happiness compared to those with higher intelligence.

When it comes to converting relations to emotions, the approach differs for introverts and extroverts. Introverts naturally limit their social circle, allowing them to be more discerning and cultivate deeper connections with others. They find solace in occasional socialization, which helps improve their well-being and prepares them for their next period of solitude. On the other hand, extroverts thrive by engaging with people, building a broad network, and forming a large community. However, even extroverts can benefit from moments of solitude and observation, providing them with a chance to recharge and find inner balance amidst their active social lives.

Please note that excessive indulgence in desires can have harmful effects. It is important to strive for a balance among the five engines. Spiritualists, in particular, may be inclined to neglect their health, spend recklessly, acquire false knowledge, and have unpredictable relationships with others. However, they easily find happiness in living in the present, taking things lightly, and not overly planning for the future. Individuals belonging to other factions can learn from this and find ways to disconnect from their long-term goals at times, embracing the joys and experiences of life's journey.

Transferring Energy to Relations

How can we effectively harness different forms of energy to nurture and strengthen our relationships? The approach may vary depending on the nature of the relationship, whether it's professional or personal.

Contributing your money through donations, charity, invitations, gifts, and active participation can greatly strengthen relationships and have a positive impact on others. Giving money may not always be a direct exchange. It can also involve hiring or demonstrating tolerance by overlooking your rights on occasion. While you may be losing money or small possessions in these situations, you are actually building stronger relationships. In official relationships, it means fulfilling your obligations such as paying taxes and other legal rights. This builds a sense of security within the legal framework and contributes to a positive reputation.

Exchanging health for relationships can manifest in various ways:

- Defending and protecting someone, even at the expense of your own well-being.
- Having less fear and worry about the outcomes of a relationship.
- Tolerating or suppressing stress, anger, and anxiety in relation to others.

These are just a few examples of how health can be used inversely to foster strong relationships with others. In official relationships, this energy transition can manifest in various ways, such as having the courage to defend your ideas or the rights of others, seeking political influence, or simply satisfying the desire for recognition. This helps to explain why the attorneys faction, which we discussed earlier, excels in swiftly navigating between relational dynamics and ensuring safety.

Converting emotions to relations involves being willing to experience discomfort so that others can feel better. We're not discussing love here, as it entails converting a relationship into an emotion. Sacrificing your own well-being can undoubtedly lead to stronger connections with others.

When you forgive someone, you resist the natural inclination for vengeance and let go of any regrets associated with it, thus opening the door for the relationship to be rebuilt. In this scenario, you will ultimately experience a sense of satisfaction when the relationship transitions back to emotions.

While learning itself can contribute to building stronger relationships in the long term by equipping you with the necessary knowledge to navigate various situations, there is also the possibility of converting learning into a relationship by focusing on less learning or simply avoiding over-analysis. While communicating with others, it's important to slow down the process of critical analysis in order to fully understand the meaning behind their feelings. After all, we are human beings, not robots.

CHAPTER 10

Execution plans

"Failing to plan is planning to fail." - Alan Lakein

Have you chosen the right goals? Are you prepared to give your all to achieve them? Keep in mind that having the will to succeed does not guarantee success. Just as you have carefully selected the right goals, it is equally important to choose the right plan. A well-crafted plan will serve as your roadmap, leading you directly towards your desired destination without wasting precious time.

Object Oriented Planning

In the field of goal engineering, much like in programming languages, humans employ two types of plans:

Class plan: This serves as the template for a plan to be executed. It defines the general structure and behavior of the plan without concerning itself with specific applications.

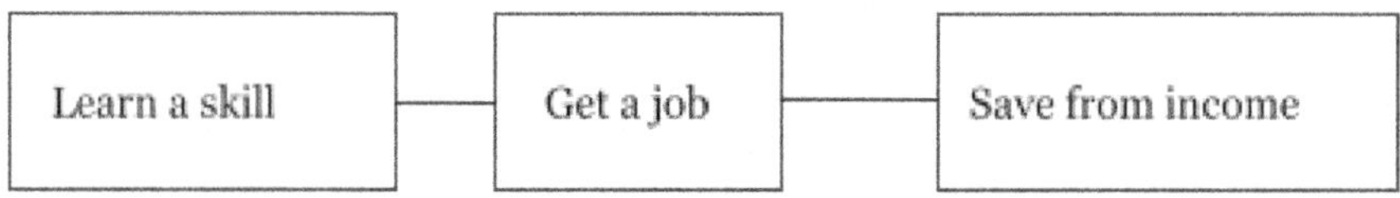

As you can observe, a class plan does not concern itself with variables such as the amount saved, job type, or skills acquired.

Object plan: It is a more specific plan and serves as a member of the class plans. From a single class type, we have the ability to generate multiple object plans by simply updating values or characteristics without altering the underlying behavior of the class plan.

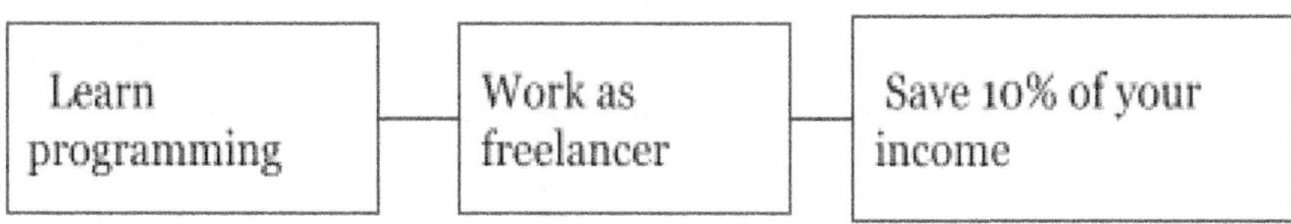

As you can observe, this object plan serves as an illustration within a vast array of plans, all crafted with the aim of attaining the common goal: financial success. However, it is crucial to note that selecting the wrong class plan will invariably impede the realization of the desired objective, except in the rare instance of fortuitous circumstances. If the foundation is flawed, any modifications made to the specific details will yield minimal impact, ultimately leaving one trapped in a cycle of failure.

Note: The class plan provided above is solely for illustrative purposes. It is not advised to implement it in your own life, as it is a misleading plan.

By selecting the appropriate class plan, you will only need to modify the parameters each time, without facing the same risks as using the wrong class plan. It becomes your responsibility to customize the given class plan in order to create a suitable object plan that aligns with your specific goals. In this chapter, we will present you with the most effective class plans that can be applied to achieve various types of goals. Additionally, we will guide you in creating accurate object plans tailored to your needs.

Financial Freedom Plans

If you want to be financially free, apply the plan represented in the figure without hesitation. This class plan suggests that the following components are essential:

- A reliable income source
- A strategy for managing expenses
- A saving strategy
- An investing strategy

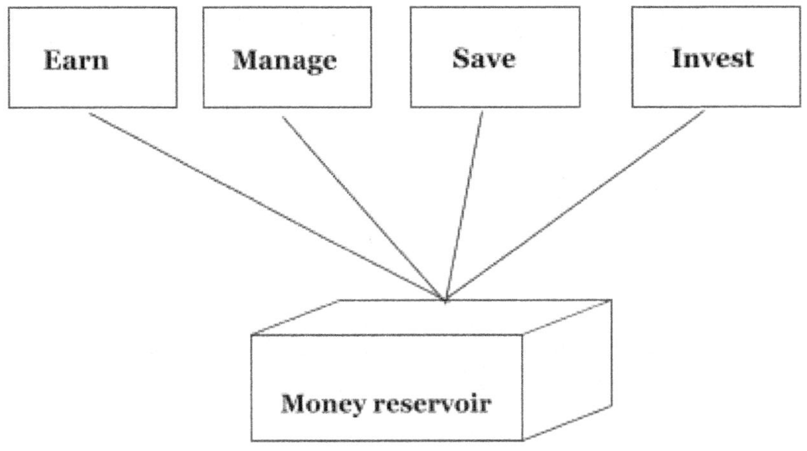

All of these components work together to fuel your financial growth. Neglecting any one of them will result in a slower pace of filling the reservoir. Now, your object plan will be influenced by your knowledge, creativity, and the choices you make. Let's take a look at some examples of different object plans.

Rich People Object Plans

Every wealthy individual is unique in their own way, but they all follow this class plan and simply modify the object plan. They prioritize long-term reservoir filling. It's important to note that saving is not a standalone component, but rather an investment with 0% interest (or even worse considering inflation). However, it plays a crucial role in leveraging investments.

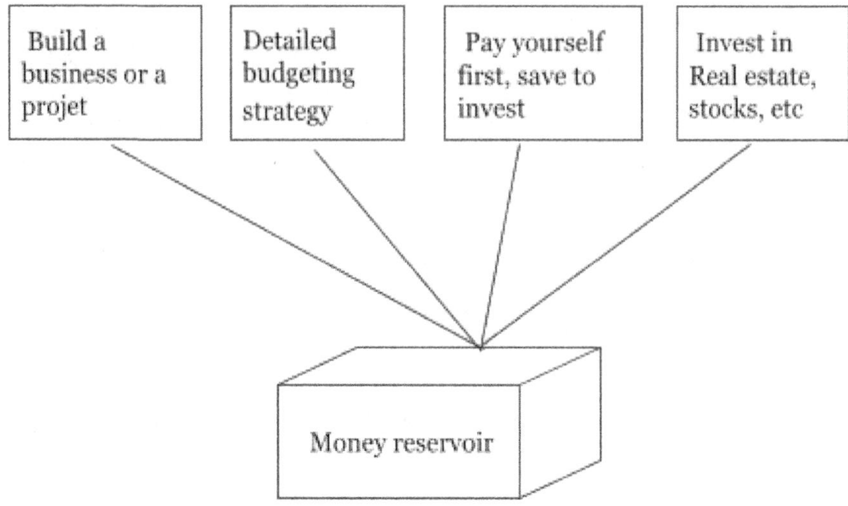

As individuals become financially successful, they may choose to simplify their plan and live differently:

1. They may stop building businesses and projects, opting for retirement.
2. They may transition into being consumers without actively managing expenses.
3. Saving money becomes less necessary as they have passive income streams.
4. They may invest in lower-risk opportunities instead of high gain risky investment.

Middle-class Financial Plans

The middle class often adheres to a common class plan and tends to adopt similar object plans. Middle-class individuals typically pursue a balanced growth strategy, aiming for high-paying jobs, implementing effective expense allocation (e.g., allocating 50% for living expenses and 10% for leisure, emergencies, etc.), saving a portion of their income (typically between 10% and 30%), and investing in what they perceive as "safe" options.

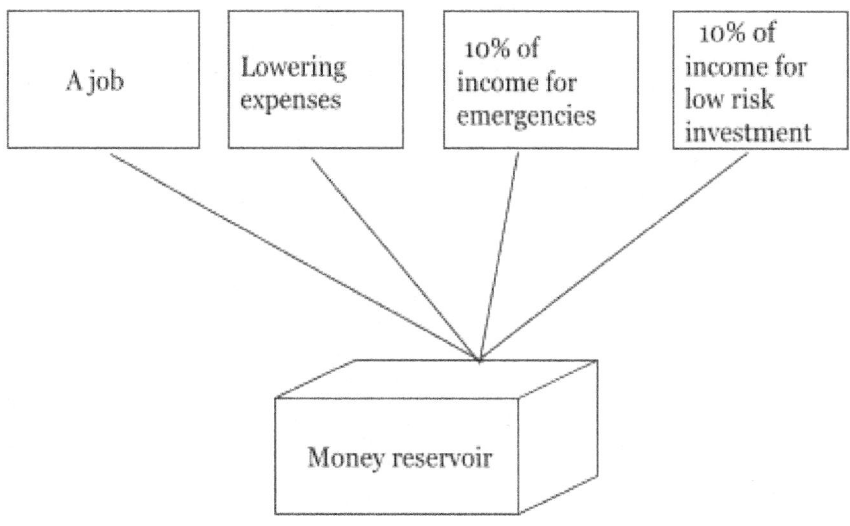

Poor's Financial Plan

Individuals in poverty often face financial struggles due to their adoption of an inadequate class plan. They frequently overlook one or more of its essential components, resulting in misguided object plans. Here's an example of a person in poverty who doesn't save money, neglects investment opportunities, and has chosen an ineffective money management strategy.

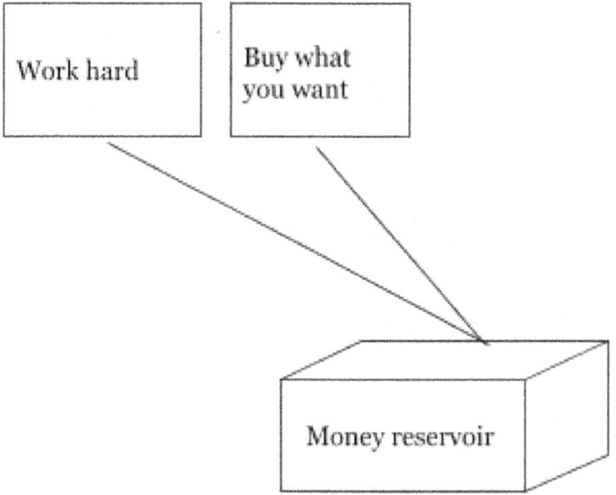

The more they neglect the essential components of the correct class plan, the greater their hardships become. Sometimes they attempt to use all four components, but not in unison. They save a substantial amount, only to later withdraw it and spend it. All of this occurs because they are adhering to the wrong template of financial freedom.

How to Create an Object Plan ?

To establish an effective object plan, it is essential to prioritize the class plan and compare its components with your innate role. Upon careful observation, you will notice that the components related to money are interconnected with other aspects of life, such as health, emotions, relationships, and knowledge. In reality, you are simply transferring energy from one form to another. It is important to recognize that money cannot be created out of thin air.

Type of energy	Activities used to generate money
Health	Work hard, use body and brain energy, get tired, sleep less.
Emotions	Control the fear of investing, resist buying temptations.
Knowledge	Invent a product or service, solve rewarding problems.
Relations	Leverage your network of relationships as a means to establish a distribution channel for your offerings.

As you can see, the prioritization of your internal goal engines will determine the specific money components you focus on during the planning and execution of your strategy. It is your responsibility to create a plan that suits your specific needs. Creating a plan for every possible scenario is beyond the scope of this book. If I were to write a book with 120 different personalities, I would provide tailored plans for each combination of engines or I would simply write another book "A plan for everything". I have given you the tools and guidance to navigate, but it is up to you to unlock the door and discover what you are capable of in the unknown.

Once you have devised and implemented your plan, your money will begin to work for you, generating additional income without the need for further input. As you transition into a consumer role, you will allocate funds towards your health, emotions, and other areas, essentially converting the energy you have accumulated back into different forms.

Getting Healthier Plans

Just like money is an energy that grows, health is a finite resource that gets consumed. Think of it as a marathon you're running. You can either maintain a steady pace to reach the finish line with less fatigue, or you can deplete your health by indulging in excessive alcohol, toxins, and unhealthy habits for the sake of momentary pleasure. The tank of health can easily be drained, so it's important to be mindful. If you've made mistakes that have negatively impacted your health, it's crucial to at least preserve what you still have.

I'm not saying that health is irreparable; you can regain it by changing your lifestyle. However, it's important to understand that the speed and amount of health you can regain is limited and proportional to the mistakes you've made. Here is the abstract class plan that you should follow, but keep in mind that the components act as valves to slow down the rate of consumption rather than directly filling the tank.

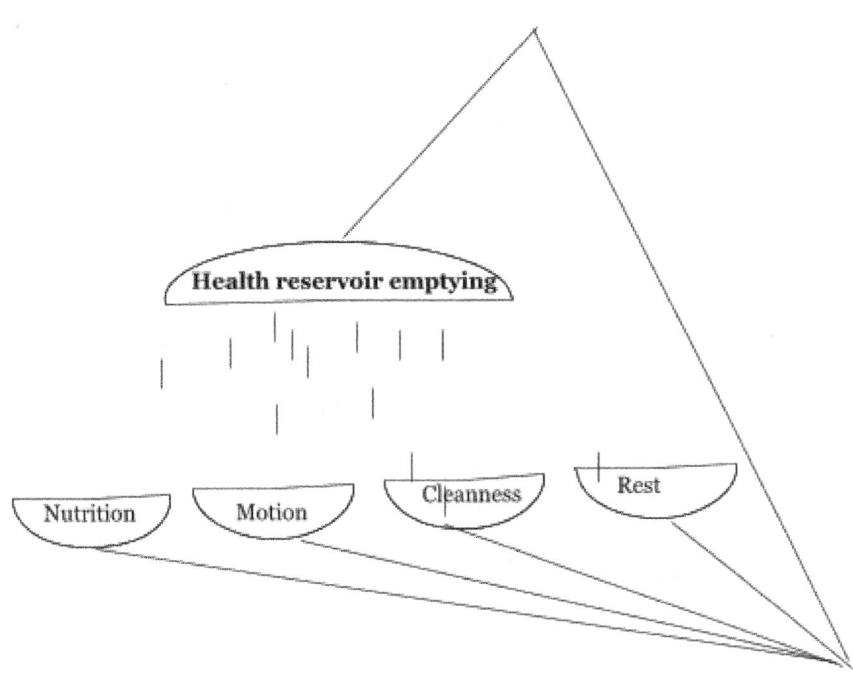

The health engine is constantly depleting its resources, while the components work to capture and replenish the lost energy back into the system. If any of the components fail to function properly, the entire system is at risk. To create an object plan you just need to instance the component. see the table below to show you different types of people and their health maintaining strategy.

Unhealthy Style

Nutrition	Eat a lot of carbohydrates Eat whatever is given
Motion	No sport Less motion, use the car to go to work
Cleanness	Utilize chemicals to mask body odor Irregular cleaning sessions
Rest	Sleep after 3 AM Sleep more than 8 hours, take a lot of naps

As you may have noticed, unhealthy styles tend to neglect or mismanage one of the four components. Opting for appropriate activities is the most effective means of implementing an object plan based on a class plan.

Healthy Style

Nutrition	• A keto diet • A low carb diet • A mediterranean diet • Diversified diet based on other parameters (season, weight ..) • Taking natural supplements and superfoods • Eating whole unprocessed foods
Motion	• Regular gym or workouts • Swimming session • 30 min walk
Cleanness	• Regular showers • Bio products for makeup and beauty • Clean environment
Rest	• Sleep at 23:00 and wake up at xx:xx..(7-8 hours) • Yoga • Meditation • 5 min rest every 30 minute work

Learning Plans

There are numerous abstract class plans available to help you acquire a wide range of skills and knowledge. Allow me to provide you with an example of an effective class plan.

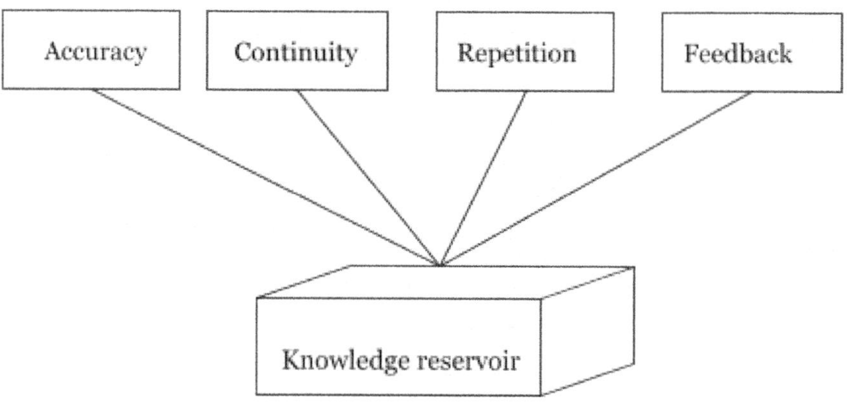

When embarking on the journey of learning any skill, be it a language, music, or physics, there are four crucial components to consider:

Accuracy of Information: It is essential to ensure the information you receive is accurate. This might involve investing in trusted sources that provide high-quality content. Free versions of courses or learning materials may contain a multitude of fallacies. Accuracy is paramount because learning false information can have long-lasting consequences that may negatively impact your life until rectified.

Continuity of learning: Consistency is key when it comes to skill development. Allocating just 10 minutes every day to practice is more effective than dedicating an hour once a week. The daily commitment allows for regular engagement and helps accelerate mastery. However, it's important to be mindful that this consistent effort may deplete your energy reserves over time. You should know how to transforme effectively your health energy effectively into knowledge.

Memory Refresh: Revising what you learn is essential, as it is akin to refilling a hole instead of simply digging it deeper. Although it may seem tedious at times, this process involves converting your emotional energy, which provides a sense of fulfillment, into valuable knowledge. Personally, I have found success with the "spaced repetition system for learning languages" and can attest to its effectiveness.

Feedback: Feedback plays a crucial role in the learning process. Without feedback, one may develop arrogance and misplaced confidence. It is important to seek feedback from experts or successful individuals who can provide valuable insights. For language learning, native speakers are particularly helpful as they can not only assess your fluency but also motivate you to improve further.

However, seeking criticism from unqualified sources can be detrimental. The same applies to learning music or singing, where the audience may not possess the same understanding as artists or specialists. Therefore, converting your relationships into knowledge effectively is essential.

Exercice :

What skill do you want to learn ?

Fill in the gaps your object plan components

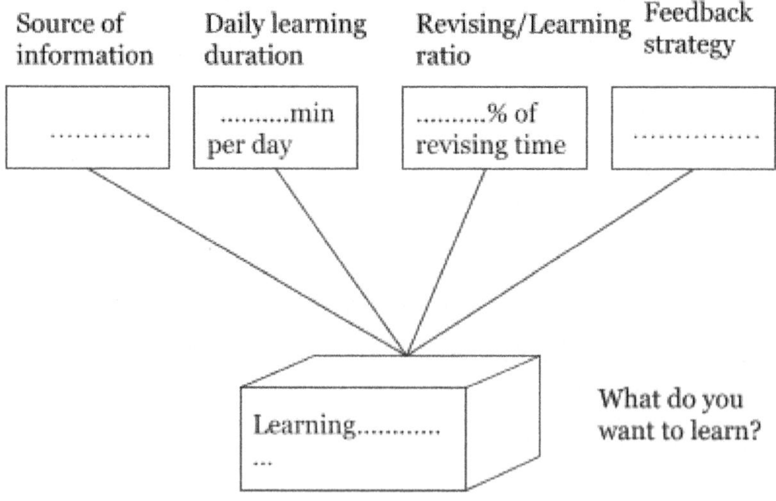

When deciding what to learn, it is crucial to consider your internal code and individual preferences. If you belong to the scholar sect, you may naturally gravitate towards exploring a wide range of complex subjects. However, individuals from other sects should strike a balance between learning what is necessary to achieve their dominant goals and pursuing their personal passions. By finding this equilibrium, you can optimize your learning experience and align it with your unique aspirations.

Feeling Better Plan

When compared to health, money, or learning plans, emotions class plans carry the least amount of long-term risk. This is because they are relatively easier to implement and adjust. If you're feeling down, you have various options to improve your mood. Simply changing your thoughts, taking a walk, meditating, playing a game, or engaging in conversation with someone can help uplift your spirits. The beauty of emotions class plans lies in their flexibility and the abundance of activities available to help you feel better.

There are numerous activities available to help you cultivate an emotional object plan. It's important to note that there isn't a one-size-fits-all approach to feeling good, as it is often centered around the present moment rather than the future. However, you can create a plan to allocate and manage your emotional energy on a daily basis, ensuring a more balanced and fulfilling experience. In reality, we simultaneously engage multiple engines, making it unclear which specific engine is directly responsible for a given activity (for further details, please refer back to Chapter 5).

Time for feeling better ....min or Hrs per day?

Class plan	Object plan (which activity do you prefer ? name yours)
Body usage (sacrificing your health or safety) .....% of leisure time	Eating? Thrill-seeking games? ....?
Ressources usage (sacrificing your money) .....% of leisure time	Shopping? Charity ? Gambling? ....?
Exploring life (effortless learning) .....% of leisure time	Gaming ? Camping? Travel? ....? ....?
Interacting with living creatures .....% of leisure time	Pets ? Friends? Family members ? ....;

Relations Building Plans

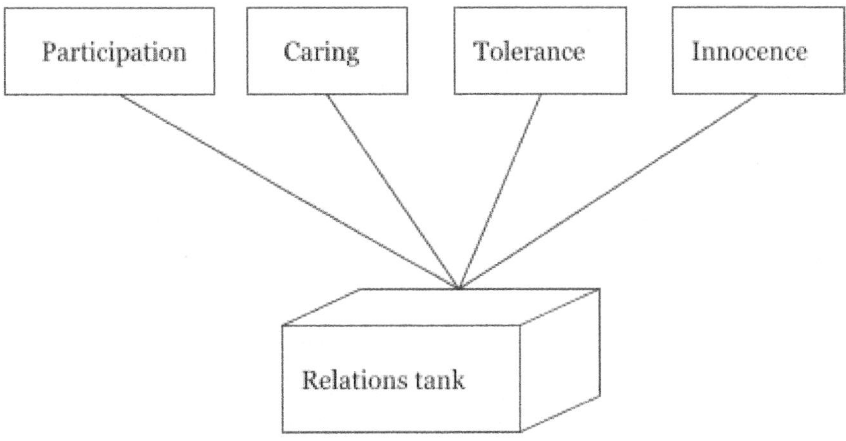

You have the flexibility to rename the components as long as you grasp the concept. Keep in mind that we are simply quantifying existing elements. When creating a flowchart for your relationship object plan, consider only activities that align with your internal goals code.

Just like with emotions, the process of creating a class or object plan involves considering the various ways energy is transferred and transformed.

- Participation involves dedicating your finances, efforts, and time to others without expecting immediate compensation.
- Caring entails prioritizing the emotions of others over your own.

- Tolerance is the willingness to accept certain risks for the sake of maintaining a healthy relationship.
- Innocence means letting go of over-analyzing and preconceived notions, and approaching others with a childlike openness and curiosity for the sake of building a better relationship.

Plans Updating

Despite carefully engineering your goals, it is inevitable to make mistakes during various steps of the process, such as categorization, ranking, planning, and more. This is a normal part of the journey, and it's important to remain flexible and embrace change after extensive deliberation. While each phase may have its own set of errors, it is crucial to make mistakes early on in the process, as executing a mistaken plan will waste your time. In fact, failure often stems from errors made during the identification phase, which is why we emphasized the importance of selecting the right goals in this book.

I hope this book has provided you with valuable insights on approaching your goals in a realistic manner. By breaking things down and understanding their underlying structure, everything becomes clear and simple. Now, it's your turn to take charge and engineer your own life. You have the concepts and tools, and you are the one who will shape your path. If you encounter any difficulties during your journey, don't hesitate to reach out to the author and his team for assistance. Until another book in this field is published, I wish you a steady and secure journey towards your success.

Thank you for reading !

Printed in Great Britain
by Amazon